HAMPSTEAD THEATRE PRESENTS THE WORLD PREMIERE OF

Love Me Tonight
by Nick Stafford

Cast (in alphabetical order)

Sarah **Amanda Abbington**
Moira **Linda Bassett**
Roy **Hugh Ross**
Stuart **Nicolas Tennant**

Director **Kathy Burke**
Designer **Bob Bailey**
Lighting **Chris Davey**
Sound **Kal Ross**

Production Manager **John Titcombe**
Technical Manager **David Tuff**
Company Stage Manager **Richard Pugh**
Deputy Stage Manager **Maggie Tully**
Assistant Stage Manager **Emma Barrow**
Chief Electrician **Greg Gould**
Deputy Chief Electrician **Chris Harris**
Costume Supervisor **Mary Charlton**

Press Representative **Emma Schad**
emmaschad@aol.com

Love Me Tonight was first performed at
Hampstead Theatre on 21 October 2004.

Hampstead Theatre
Eton Avenue
Swiss Cottage
London
NW3 3EU

Tickets & information
020 7722 9301
www.hampsteadtheatre.com
info@hampsteadtheatre.com

The Company

Nick Stafford Writer

Nick Stafford has written extensively for theatre and has been the writer in residence at the Half Moon Young People's Theatre, the Young Vic and Birmingham Repertory Theatre. His theatre work includes **Luminosity** (Royal Shakespeare Company); **Battle Royal** (National Theatre); **The Devil's Only Sleeping**; **The Whisper of Angel's Wings** and **The Snow Queen**.

As a screenplay writer, Nick won the Dennis Potter Award for **Pity**. His latest screenplay is **The Girl He Left Behind**, developed through PAL.

Nick has also written several radio plays for BBC Radio 4, including adaptations of the novels **Birdsong, A Thousand Acres** and **Frankenstein**, and **The List**, two plays written to commemorate VE day. His radio play **A Matter of Sex** won the Sony Award for the Best Original Script.

Amanda Abbington Sarah

Theatre includes: **The Safari Party** (Scarborough / Hampstead Theatre); Something Blue (Scarborough); **Taming of the Shrew** (Queen Mother Theatre) and **Tin Soldiers** (New End Theatre / Grace Theatre).

Television includes: The Robinsons, **Teachers, Coupling, Bernard's Watch, 20 Things To Do Before You're 30, The Debt, A & E, Hearts and Bones II, Men Only, Shaeds, Sins, Dream Team, The Thing About Vince, Snap, The Bill, Casualty, Picking Up The Pieces, Wycliffe, No Sweat, Magic** and **Plotlands.**

Films includes: **Slip Road.**

Linda Bassett Moira

Theatre includes, for the Royal Court: **Lucky Dog, Far Away, East is East** (co-production with Tamasha: Birmingham Rep / tour / Theatre Royal, Stratford East); **Our Country's Good, The Recruiting Officer, Serious Money** (Public Theatre New York); **Aunt Dan and Lemon, Abel's Sister** and **Fen** (Joint Stock / tour / Public Theatre New York).

Other theatre includes: **Richard III, The Taming of the Shrew** (Globe); **Five Kinds of Silence** (Lyric Hammersmith); **The Dove** (Croydon Warehouse); **The Triumph of Love** (Almeida / tour); **The Clearing** (Bush); **Henry IV parts 1 & 2, The Theban Plays, Artists and Admirers** (Royal Shakespeare Company); **The Awakening, Out in the Open** (Hampstead Theatre); **Schism in England, Juno and the Paycock, A Place with the Pigs** (National Theatre); **The Seagull** (Liverpool Playhouse); **George Dandin, Medea, Woyceck, Bald Prima Donna** (Leicester Haymarket / Liverpool Playhouse / Almeida Theatre); **Falkland Sound** (Belgrade Coventry); **The Cherry Orchard** (Leicester Haymarket) and **John Gabriel Borkman** (English Touring Theatre). Work with Interplay Community Theatre. Work in Belgrade Theatre-in-Education Company, Coventry.

Film includes: **Waiting for the Moon, Leave to Remain, Indian Summer, Oscar and Lucinda, East is East, Beautiful People, The Martins, The Hours, Spivs, A Way through the Woods** and **Calendar Girls**.

Television includes: **Bramwell, Loved Up, Cold Light of Day, Skallagrig, A Touch of Frost, A Small Dance, Newshounds, Christmas, No Bananas, Casualty, Kavanagh QC, Silent Film, Far from the Madding Crowd, Spoonface Steinberg, The Life & Crimes of William Palmer, Our Mutual Friend, Out of Hours** and **The Brief**.

Awards include: Best Actress Award Senana Internacional de Cine Valladolid Espania, nominated Best Actress London Evening Standard British Film Awards, and nomination for Best Actress in the BAFTA Awards 2000 **(East is East)**.

Hugh Ross Roy

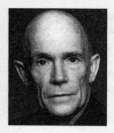

Hugh trained at the Royal Academy of Dramatic Art.

Theatre includes: **The David Hare Trilogy** (Birmingham Repertory Theatre); **A Prayer for Owen Meany, Battle Royal, Lady in the Dark** (National Theatre); **The Woman in Black** (Fortune Theatre); **Fifty Revolutions** (Whitehall Theatre); **Invention of Love** (Theatre Royal Haymarket); **Passion** (Olivier Award nomination, Queen's Theatre London); **Tartuffe** (Royal Exchange, Manchester); **Democracy** (Bush Theatre); **Dr Faustus, Mary Stuart** (Greenwich Theatre); **King Lear** (Royal Court); **Death and the Maiden** (Duke of York's); **Hedda Gabler** (Playhouse Theatre); **As You Like It, All's Well That Ends Well** (Stratford / Barbican); **Bussy D'Ambois** (Old Vic); **Twelfth Night** and **The Cid** (London / tour).

Film includes: **Charlotte Gray, The Four Feathers, The Tell-Tale Heart, Gooseberries Don't Dance, Trainspotting, Patriot Games** and **Nightbreed**.

Television includes: **Mine All Mine, Sea of Souls, Snoddy, Dead Souls, Cazalet Chronicle, Men Only, Mists of Avalon, Invasion Earth, Family Money, Sharpe's Sword, Sharpe's Battle, Sharpe's Gold, Dr Finlay, Between the Lines, Lovejoy, Absolutely Fabulous, An Ungentlemanly Act, Poirot, The Advocates** and **Misterioso**.

Audio: Over 100 radio plays. For the BBC Shakespeare Collection, **Twelfth Night, Julius Caesar**; For Arkangel Shakespeare, **Macbeth**; For Chivers Books, **Midsomer Murders**.

As a director: **The Glass Menagerie** (Tower Theatre); **Stevie** (Mercury, Colchester) and **After Liverpool** (Royal Shakespeare Company).

Nicolas Tennant Stuart

Theatre includes: **Cloud 9, Teeth n Smiles** (Sheffield); **Taming of the Shrew Tamer Tamed, King Lear** (RSC); **The Associate, The Blue Ball, Billy Liar** (National Theatre); **A Christmas Carol** (Chichester); **Comedians** (Oxford Stage Company); **Action** (Young Vic); **Herons** (Royal Court); **Les Justes** (Gate Theatre); **The Recruiting Officer** (Chichester Festival Theatre); **Little Malcolm and his Struggle Against the Eunuchs** (Hampstead Theatre); **A Carpet, A Pony, and A Monkey; Sugar, Sugar, Love and Understanding** (Bush Theatre); **New Play Festival** (Derby Playhouse); **Henry IV** (English Touring Theatre / Old Vic); **Not a Game for Boys** (Not the National Theatre Tour / Edinburgh Festival) and **Bad Company** (National Theatre Studio / Bush Theatre).

Films include: **Sex Lives of the Potato Men, Tube Tales, Oscar and Lucinda, Backbeat, The Gift, The Fool** and **A Dangerous Man.**

Television includes: **Residents, The Bombmaker, Friday on my Mind** and **Nice Town.**

Kathy Burke Director

Theatre directing credits include: **The Quare Fellow** by Brendan Behan (Oxford Stage Company); **Born Bad** by Debbie Tucker Green and **Out in the Open** by Jonathan Harvey (Hampstead Theatre); **Betty** by Karen McLachlan (Vaudeville Theatre); **Kosher Harry** by Nick Grosso (Royal Court); **Boom Bang-a-Bang** by Jonathan Harvey (Bush Theatre) and **Mr Thomas by Kathy Burke** (Old Red Lion and Channel 4).

Bob Bailey Designer

Bob Bailey trained at Central St Martins College of Art and Design

Current and recent work: **Cabaret** (English Theatre, Frankfurt); **The Lieutenant of Inishmore** (Fiery Angel UK tour); **The Godbotherers** (Bush Theatre); **Tosca** (Nationale Reisopera, Holland); **The Lying Kind** (Royal Court Theatre), **Stitching** (Traverse, Edinburgh, Bush Theatre & UK / European tour).

Previous productions include: **Angels in America** (Crucible Theatre, Sheffield); Hijrah (Bush / Plymouth), **Venecia** (Gate Theatre); All Nighter, **Horseplay** (Royal Ballet), **Aeroplane Man** (Stratford East), **Sweeney Todd, The Baker's Wife, A Little Night Music** (Royal Academy of Music); **Edward Gant's Amazing Feats of Loneliness** (Drum, Plymouth).

In 1999 Bob won the Time Out Designer of the Year Award for **The Happiest Day of My Life** (DV8 Dance Company UK/European Tour).

Chris Davey Lighting

Chris Davey's designs for Hampstead Theatre include **Yellowman, Sunday Father** and **Out in the Open**. He has also designed extensively for West Yorkshire Playhouse, Royal Exchange Manchester, Royal Lyceum Edinburgh, Traverse Edinburgh, Birmingham Rep, Tamasha Theatre, Oxford Stage Company, Shared Experience, the RSC and the Royal Court.

Other designs include: **Iphigenia at Aulis** (National Theatre); **Flew Over The Cuckoos Nest** (Edinburgh Festival 2004 / West End); **The Quare Fellow** (Oxford Stage Company); **Beasts and Beauties** (Bristol Old Vic); **Rattle of a Simple Man** (Comedy Theatre); **The Taming of the Shrew, The Deep Blue Sea** (national tour); **After Mrs Rochester** (Shared Experience / Duke of York); ; **21** (Rambert Dance Company); **Romeo and Juliet** (Chichester Festival); **The Vagina Monologues** (national tour); **My One and Only** (Piccadilly / Chichester); **Dangerous Corner** (Garrick); **Jekyll and Hyde** (Northern Ballet Theatre); **The Car Man** (AMP); **Closer** (Abbey Dublin) and **Baby Doll** (Albery / National Theatre / Birmingham Rep).

His opera includes: **Jephtha** (Welsh National Opera); three seasons with Grange Park Opera; **The Picture of Dorian Gray** (Opera de Monte Carlo); **La Traviata** (Castleward Opera Belfast).

Kal Ross Sound

Sound designs include: **The Lonesome West, Brothers of the Brush, Ballad of the Sea, The Knocky, Happy Valley, Scouse - A Comedy of Terrors** (Liverpool Everyman); **Educating Rita, Romeo & Juliet, Popcorn, Les Liasons Dangereuses, Playboy of the Western World, Oliver Twist, A Christmas Carol, Sergeant Pepper's Magical Mystery Trip** (Liverpool Playhouse); **Thick as a Brick, Gold** (Hull Truck Theatre); **Jungle Book** (Chester Gateway); **The Play What I Wrote (Wyndhams); In Other Words** (UK tour), later to become **The Singing Playwrights** (Pleasance Grand, Edinburgh); **The Corrupted Angel** (Bass Chorus / tour); **Celtic Rhythm US Tour, The Starving Brides** (HUB / tour) **and Words on the Run** (tour).

With the creation of new company CM2r, Kal has recently returned to co-writing, recording and producing music in collaboration with bands and artistes from up and down the UK.

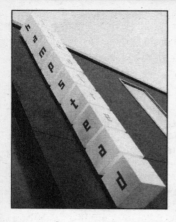

Over the past forty years Hampstead Theatre has established a unique reputation for the ambition, quality and success of the new plays it has produced.

Writers who have premiered work at Hampstead Theatre include Michael Frayn, Harold Pinter, David Edgar, Terry Johnson, Mike Leigh, Timberlake Wertenbaker, Philip Ridley, Shelagh Stephenson, Hanif Kureishi, Tamsin Oglesby, Simon Block, Abi Morgan and Debbie Tucker Green to name but a few.

Unlike other new writing theatres in London, Hampstead Theatre has always sought to reflect the concerns and aspirations of those communities living in easy reach of the theatre, as well as making a distinct contribution to the national and international scene.

In 2003 the company moved into a brand new, award winning building that stands at the heart of the Swiss Cottage Centre Development. The building comprises two venues: a flexible 325 seat auditorium and a studio, The Space, dedicated exclusively to education work. In its first year in the new building, the company has successfully extended the range of its programme to increase the size and broaden the diversity of its audience. The education programme has attracted over 18,000 attendances. The spring season saw sell out performances of Hanif Kureishi's **When the Night Begins**, and Alistair Beaton's satire, **Follow My Leader**. The European premiere of Dael Orlandersmith's **Yellowman** had people rising to their feet.

With our autumn season of plays, our Start Nights and our extensive education programme both in and outside the building, we will build on this success.

Become a Priority Supporter

With advance information and priority booking you can be the first to discover fresh and dynamic playwrights, and make the most of a range of discounts for just £12 a year. For more details call us on **020 7722 9301** or email info@hampsteadtheatre.com

Hampstead Theatre's Education & Participation Programme

Based in The Space, a fully flexible performance area in the new theatre, local residents and schools make use of our expertise and facilities though a number of different projects.

The Heat and Light Company brings together 11 – 23 years olds to explore and make theatre. Five different groups offer the opportunity to develop playwriting, performing, directing, designing and technical skills, with nine different new plays produced and performed each year.

Ignite covers a range of workshops organised with local schools. These include breakfast, lunch and after school clubs that offer an introduction to theatre skills. In addition a full programme of teacher training and production related workshops is available to support productions.

Generator provides members from a wide variety of backgrounds, experiences, cultures and ages with a means to join together and express themselves creatively.

Run in collaboration with the Swiss Cottage Community Centre, the **Older Writers group** aims to develop the playwriting skills of those over 60.

ESOL - for students for whom English is not their first language work to build their confidence and develop their language skills with drama games and workshops held in The Space.

Our monthly **Start Nights** bring The Space to life every month with a selection of new writers from London, testing out material in front of a live audience. around the world.

For more information on any of our projects or about how to join any of our participation programmes, visit our website, talk to us on 020 7449 4165 or email education@hampsteadtheatre.com

'A splendid new home for new writing'

Support Hampstead Theatre

Luminaries

By becoming one of Hampstead Theatre's Luminaries, you will be giving vital support to all aspects of our work, and become more involved with the theatre. There are three levels of support and a variety of benefits offered including priority booking, a dedicated booking line, crediting in playtexts and programmes and invitations to exclusive events. Membership starts at £250 per year.

Our **Luminaries** are:

Level 1
Anonymous, Michael & Leslie Bennett, Denis & Ronda Cassidy, Frankie de Freitas, Robyn Durie, George Fokschaner, Richard Gladstone, Elaine & Peter Hallgarten, Patricia and Jerome Karet, Tom & Karen Mautner, Judith Mishon & Philip Mishon OBE, Sandy & David Montague, Trevor Phillips, Tamara & Michael Rabin, Sue and Lionel Rosenblatt, Peter Roth QC, Barry Serjent, Dr Michael Spiro, Hugh Whitemore & Rohan McCulloch, Adrian Whiteson

Level 2
Dorothy & John Brook, Professor & Mrs C J Dickinson, Matthew & Alison Green, The Mackintosh Foundation, Midge & Simon Palley, Michael & Olivia Prior, Anthony Rosner, Judy Williams

Level 3
Sir Trevor Chinn, David Dutton, Jacqueline and Jonathan Gestetner, Sir Eddie Kulukundis OBE, Daniel Peltz, Richard Peskin, Wendy and Peter Phillips, Paul Rayden

If there is a particular area of our work that you would like to support, please talk to us. We have numerous projects available covering all aspects of our work from education to play development.

Why not consider leaving a legacy to the theatre? This gives us lasting support well into the future. You can leave a gift to support a new commission, to fund education work or leace it open for us to use it in the area of most need.

Corporate Partners

Hampstead Theatre's Corporate Partnersscheme offers a flexible package of benefits with which you can entertain your clients, promote your business objectives, provide benefits to your staff and take advantage of everything that the theatre has to offer. Corporate Partners membership is available from £5,000 + VAT.

Our current Corporate Partners are:

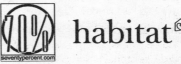

We offer a range of other sponsorship opportunities, from performance sponsorship, project support, production sponsorship, gala event sponsorship, support for our education work or even title sponsorship for the entire season. Benefits can be tailored to your needs – please talk to us for more information.

Hampstead Theatre's Supporters - 2003/04

Abbey National Charitable Foundation – Supporting Sign Interpreted Performances, ADAPT Trust – Barry Foster Memorial. Award for, Excellence in Access, 2003, Arts & Business New Partners, Auerbach Trust Charity, Bridge House Estates Trust Fund, The City Parochial Foundation, The Clothworkers Foundation, John Lyon's Charitable Trust, The John S Cohen Foundation, Lloyds TSB Foundation for England and Wales, Mildred Duveen Trust, Moose Foundation for the Arts, The Paul Hamlyn Foundation, The Rayne Foundation, Reed Elsevie

For more information on any of these or if you would like to support the theatre in another way, please contact Sarah Coop in the Development Department on 020 7449 4160 or email development@hampsteadtheatre.com

As a registered charity, Hampstead Theatre can accept donations from charitable trusts and foundations, gifts of stocks and shares, donations via CAF America or in a tax-efficient manner under the Gift Aid Scheme.

Nick Stafford
Love Me Tonight

faber and faber

First published in 2004
by Faber and Faber Limited
3 Queen Square London WC1N 3AU
Published in the United States by Faber and Faber Inc.
an affiliate of Farrar, Straus and Giroux LLC, New York

Typeset by Country Setting, Kingsdown, Kent CT14 8ES
Printed in England by Mackays of Chatham plc, Chatham, Kent

A CIP record for this book
is available from the British Library

ISBN 0-571-22726-0

2 4 6 8 10 9 7 5 3 1

Characters

Roy
mid-fifties

Moira
a bit younger

Sian
their daughter, thirtyish

Stuart
their son, thirtyish

Act One

*The sound of waves. Lights up on a good-sized kitchen to
the rear of a house on a seashore in the south of England.
There is furniture, but no large table dominates. There
are doorways into the house and to the outside.*

*Enter Roy, from inside. He's dressed in a black suit and
tie. He pours himself a Scotch from a secret bottle, rests
a beat, gulps it with ease. He exits to inside.*

*Enter Sian, from inside, also dressed in black, carrying
dirty plates, etc. She and Roy cross.*

Sian Dad?

Roy They've seen off all five boxes of white, you know?
Fifteen litres! Good job we didn't buy ten boxes or they'd
be here all night.

*He exits, Sian puts the plates down. Enter Stuart from
inside, dressed in black, carrying dirty plates, etc.*

Stuart Thank God they've nearly all gone. (*adding his
plates to Sian's*) Just two old ladies that no one seems to
know, and Dr Godsave . . . (*He looks for a reaction from
Sian.*) How do you think Mum and Dad are?

Sian My professional opinion?

Stuart Professional!

Sian They're grieving.

Stuart Of course. Are you staying tonight?

Sian Yes, are you?

Stuart I'm not fit to drive anywhere.

Sian I thought Auntie Pat might stay.

Stuart That'd be a first. Vince's GCSE results came today.

Sian No.

Stuart Five As, two Bs and an unclassified.

Sian What was the unclassified?

Stuart History.

Sian He hated history.

Stuart Dad says he and Mum are buying a camper van and going off.

Sian When did he say that?

Stuart Today. In the Gents at the crematorium.

Sian Going off for how long?

Stuart He's thinking of taking early retirement.

Sian And Mum?

Neither sees Roy arrive in the doorway to inside with dirty plates, etc.

Stuart I'm not sure he's actually told Mum he's thinking of retiring or that they're going off together –

Enter Roy.

Roy When a man tells another man something while they're shoulder-to-shoulder at a urinal it's usually in confidence. But I forgive you. It's going to be good. No, it's going to be great. (*opening first bottle of red wine*) It's what everyone dreams of. One of the things. One of the things they say they dream of. Not everyone; but I have, I do. Pack it all in.

Stuart Why work all your life?

6

Roy Exactly. Have either of you sorted out your long-term finances yet? Do it. I mean it. You, especially.

Stuart I'm thinking about it.

Roy 'I'm thinking about it.' Do it. Pension plans, etcetera. What about Little Charlie?

Stuart He's a bit young to be thinking of a pension, but I've started a savings plan for when he's twenty-one.

Roy How much?

Stuart Ten pounds a month. Not much, but tax free.

Roy What about life cover?

Stuart For who?

Roy On you, for him and Sue.

Stuart I can't decide what I'm worth.

Roy It's calculated on your income.

Stuart Not a lot, then.

Roy Do it.

Stuart No.

Roy No?

Stuart I'm thinking about it.

Enter Moira from inside, in black, carrying nothing.

Roy The longer you leave it, the more expensive the premiums. And it costs more if you're a smoker.

Roy pours Moira a red wine.

Stuart Is that your way of asking if I've given up?

Moira Have you?

Stuart Yes.

7

Moira Good.

Roy Not before time.

Stuart Hark to the chorus of self-righteous ex-smokers.

Roy That's us; now we have all the information about the harmful effects. Everyone gone?

Moira Yes.

Roy Sit down. You've been on your feet all day.

Moira doesn't sit.

Sian Who were the two old ladies?

Roy They attend funerals, apparently. Dr Godsave's giving them a lift.

Stuart Did you smoke when you were pregnant?

Moira No.

Stuart No?

Roy She puked for nine months with all three of you. Couldn't face the fags.

Moira But I had a cigarette as soon as I could. As soon as I felt well enough.

Sian This house stank of smoke.

Moira It was normal, then. Everyone smelt stale.

Roy Including you two, who thought we didn't notice you were stealing cigarettes from us. Do you ever smoke now?

Sian Only cannabis.

Roy Is that a joke?

Sian No.

8

Moira How's Little Charlie?

Stuart Lovely. Sends his love.

Moira Is he coming to see us, soon?

Stuart Yeah. I didn't think he'd understand today. He shouts a lot at the moment.

The first bottle of red wine is emptied by Roy into his own glass, which he then drains.

Roy All gone? Chilean. Lovely. Bought it at a wine-tasting.

Moira Do you taste it?

Sian Cannabis is a better drug than alcohol because it frees you but doesn't give you a hangover.

Roy Yes, it does.

Stuart How do you know?

Roy There was a debate on daytime TV. I'll open another one, shall I?

Sian I've never had a hangover from cannabis. (*A beat.*) What?

Roy Nothing.

Sian What?

Moira Nothing.

Sian You're looking at me.

Moira Cannabis.

Roy I can't decide – another Chilean? A French? A Spanish? A nice Rioja? Which one?

Stuart holds up a bottle.

That one?

Moira (*shrugs*) They're all nice.

Sian That one.

Stuart Yes?

Roy Good choice. (*Opens the bottle, pours.*)

Stuart Yes, yep. Yep, yep. Bouquet, taste, etcetera.

Roy (*pours for Moira*) Sian?

Sian Half a glass.

Stuart Don't want to mix your drugs.

Moira Wine isn't a drug.

Sian It's not legally classified as such, no.

Moira It is nice.

Roy It is rather good.

Moira A sort of nice after-thing.

Stuart Sort of nice?

Moira Yes.

Stuart After-thing?

Moira Yes.

   Beats.

Stuart (*to Roy*) 'How did you get here?' You haven't asked me that, today. (*to Sian*) Did he ask you?

Roy Lie for me.

Sian No.

Stuart No, you won't lie, or no, he didn't ask you?

Roy Yes, I did ask her.

Stuart Did you tell him?

Sian No.

Stuart You refused?

Sian He didn't wait for the answer. It was chit-chat.

Stuart Do you want to know how I got here?

Roy No.

Stuart Yes, you do.

Roy No, I don't.

Stuart Okay.

Roy 'How did you get here?' is a request for information. You get the answer, then you can imagine the journey. What landmarks, what features, what perils the traveller has encountered. It's interesting.

Stuart (*to Moira*) Is it, Mum?

Moira I like hearing the answer.

Stuart But you've never asked the question. Is that because Dad's always asked it or because you couldn't be bothered?

Moira I've not really thought about it.

Roy It's not really worth the bother thinking about it. It's just something that somebody does.

Stuart It's not something that somebody does, it's what *you* do.

Moira He used to tell me that he felt he hovered over you on your –

Roy No, I didn't –

Stuart You obviously did, because you're interrupting before she could say what you fear she was about to.

Moira He felt he hovered over you all.

Stuart You've embarrassed him.

Sian Do you still do it?

Roy Do what?

Stuart But you did do it?

Roy I've got better things to do with my time.

Sian What did you see?

Stuart Could you see us? Hang on – if he could see us, why did he ask how we got here?

Sian Perhaps he could only track one of us at a time.

Stuart Did you see us, like, all the time? Doing everything? . . . He's not going to tell us.

Moira You're teasing him.

Roy They're teasing me?

Sian He can't have seen everything I did or I wouldn't be here now.

Stuart Nor me.

Roy I wouldn't've wanted to have seen everything.

Sian I'd watch someone if I could without them knowing.

Stuart Some unknowing stranger?

Sian Fly on the wall.

Stuart Dad in the air.

Sian If someone told you that you could secretly watch someone every second, doing everything –

Roy Boring. It'd be boring, most of it. More boring than Daytime TV or *Big Brother* –

Stuart They know they're being watched –

Sian Someone could edit the boring bits out.

Roy And you could put them on daytime TV. Actually, I think that's what they do now.

Stuart No, you'd have to watch everything, because someone else might edit the stuff they think's boring but you find fascinating.

Moira If you spent all your time watching someone there wouldn't be any time for yourself.

The other three realise Moira's just told them off.
A beat.

Stuart When Charlie was just born I watched him all the time.

Moira Well, he is lovely.

Stuart I tell him now, these are the carefree days of your life. Savour them.

Sian Does he understand?

Stuart Who knows? He nods; he looks grave. That grave look of his.

Roy When you tell him, 'These are the carefree days of your life, savour them,' do you tell him like that, like you just demonstrated?

Stuart Like what?

Roy Like you just did.

Stuart How did I just do?

Roy Gravely. No wonder he's grave; you're grave.

Stuart I'm grave as in serious.

Roy You're telling him that these are the happiest days of your life with a face like –

Stuart I didn't say 'happiest'. I said 'carefree'.

Roy You meant happiest.

Stuart I did not. I meant what I said – carefree – and when I say he looks grave I mean he looks – I mean I know that he's taking me seriously. He understands it's important to be carefree.

Roy It's not a question of importance, is it? He just is carefree because he hasn't any cares, yet. He's free of cares –

Stuart No, we've worked at that –

Roy He's two years old, he has a normal sort of life, therefore he's relatively free of cares –

Stuart We've worked at it that he's carefree.

Moira (*cutting Roy out*) You and Sue?

Stuart Yes, me and Sue.

 A beat.

Sian Does Charlie know what you're doing here today?

Stuart Not really. One day he'll ask, 'Where's Vince?' I've told him Vince has died.

Roy You told him?

Stuart Yes.

Roy Was that wise?

Stuart You obviously think not.

Roy I just don't like to think of Little Charlie being upset.

Stuart He wasn't upset.

Roy He wasn't upset that Vince had gone?

Stuart I didn't say Vince had gone; I said he'd died.

Owing mostly to Roy, the second bottle of red wine is empty.

Roy Another?

Stuart Why not?

Roy Four people isn't much for a bottle of wine.

Moira I think you mean that vice versa.

Stuart A bottle of wine isn't very much for four people.

Roy Shall I choose?

Moira Go on.

Roy Lighter or heavier?

Moira Whichever.

Roy Stronger or weaker?

Moira Whichever.

Roy We've got twelve per cent, twelve and a half per cent, or a whopping fourteen.

Stuart Is that how they were presented at the wine tasting?

Roy No, the judging criteriia were: first, label; and only second, percentage alcohol. Third, taste. (*He opens the third bottle and fills the glasses.*) Third was taste.

There are sips and glances and looks out towards the darkness of the sea and the sky.

Stuart Cheers.

Roy Cheers.

Sian *Salut.*

Roy How's things?

Sian Fine.

Roy Work?

Sian Fine

Roy Romance?

Sian The same. What?

Stuart What?

Sian What were you doing?

Moira He was mouthing.

Stuart I kind of knew what was coming next.

Sian No, you didn't, actually.

Roy I thought we might buy a camper van.

Sian and Stuart just catch the reaction Moira covers.

Drive about a bit. Follow our fancy.

Stuart And go camping?

Roy In a van.

Stuart On campsites?

Roy A big van. A proper one. Follow the sun.

Stuart Abroad?

Roy Don't know. (*to Stuart*) You could come along and bring Little Charlie.

Stuart Where to?

Roy Don't know; anywhere.

Stuart We'd have to know where we were going. And for how long. I couldn't say to Sue that we were travelling for an unspecified amount of time to an unnamed destination.

Roy That'd be too carefree, perhaps?

Moira Have you looked at any vans?

Roy Yes.

Moira Driven any?

Roy No. Well, yes. A couple. Does everyone still like this wine?

Sian Where's it from?

Roy (*covering label*) Tesco's.

Sian I meant what country?

Roy It's a cheeky little number, from guess?

Stuart Spain.

Sian Sicily.

Roy Not a country . . . Moira?

Moira shrugs.

It's perky. It's young. It's last year's . . . It's Cretan!
It passes all three wine tests with flying colours: great label, great percentage alcohol, and not a bad –

Moira deliberately knocks her wine over and watches it spread.

Sian Are you okay?

Moira Yes.

Sian Taken any pills today?

Moira Yes.

Roy fills a new glass for Moira. She takes a sip.

Stuart (*to Moira*) I was thinking about that couple at the end of Stone Road, in that cul-de-sac that was built when me and Sian were small.

Moira Which couple?

Stuart He was building a yacht. She died.

Moira The Hudsons. Peter and Janey.

Stuart They were going to sail around the world, weren't they?

Moira Were they?

Stuart In the boat he was making. What did she die of?

Moira A stroke. She was talking to her husband and she dropped dead and he thought she was playing a joke. Apparently she liked practical jokes.

Stuart What happened to him and his boat?

Roy What's this? 'Twenty questions about the Hudsons'?

Stuart Nowhere near twenty. (*responding to Sian*) What's up? What's the matter?

Moira Peter Hudson went off alone.

Roy (*cutting across*) How's work, Sian?

Stuart would like to continue on the Hudsons, but Moira seems indifferent.

Sian Good.

Roy What's your latest thing?

Sian Thing?

Roy You know – method.

Sian My latest thing is called Deep Tissue Therapy.

Stuart Sponsored by Kleenex?

Sian Fna, fna. The philosophy behind Deep Tissue Therapy is that our experiences are not just stored in our memory, but in our body. There is a physical response to experience that lingers long after the actual experience has ceased, an emotional response which is stored in the body. A deformity ensues. Ossified memories create a list in the body, a twist, a distortion, a tightness. We find lumps, knots: ossified tissue. Shall I demonstrate? (*She precisely positions her thumbs on her brother, then applies pressure.*)

Stuart Jesus!

Sian I hardly touched you.

Roy That's good for you?

Sian Sometimes thumbs aren't enough. Sometimes it's elbows.

Stuart Who invented this therapy – General Pinochet?

Roy Are you all right?

Stuart She's left a mark.

Sian You jerked away.

Stuart Too right.

Sian Did any memories come up?

Roy People volunteer for that?

Sian They do.

Roy And pay money?

Stuart The kind of people who squeeze themselves into latex lederhosen come the weekend?

Sian Inside the mouth is the most interesting place.

Stuart In the mouth?

Sian Did you jerk away from a memory?

Stuart I jerked away from a pain.

Roy Fingers and thumbs in the mouth?

Sian Look how tight our jaws are.

Roy They'd fall open if they weren't a bit tight. We'd all look stupid. People who forget their mouths are open look stupid. Like this. I bet I look positively moronic. Try it.

No one else does.

Stuart It's because you're doing something with your eyes as well.

Roy I'll try and leave the mouth open but keep the eyes alive . . . See, can't do it.

Sian Anyway. Ossified experiences can be released . . . Mum, Dad? Fancy a go?

They both demur.

Stuart – let me do you properly, I'd only just laid hands on you.

Stuart (*holding up third bottle of red wine*) Half-empty, by God.

Moira How much are you drinking?

Stuart When?

Moira Generally.

Roy Your mother's worried because of Auntie Miriam –

Moira And because of your father –

Roy Gin was her tipple, wasn't it?

Moira Mostly.

Roy I don't touch the stuff. She pickled her liver – can't do that with wine.

Moira Can't you?

Roy Not as easily.

Sian Was Aunt Miriam yellow?

Moira She was yellow.

Sian As yellow as Vince?

Roy I don't drink any spirits. Just wine with food. And without.

Stuart Do you take Valium every day?

Moira Sometimes.

Stuart Is Dr Godsave your GP?

Moira In this, yes.

Stuart He's just your GP for Valium?

Moira He's prescribed me Valium, yes.

Stuart I never knew his first name was Philip.

Moira Didn't you?

Stuart How much notice do you have to give?

Moira In respect of what?

Stuart Leaving Dr Godsave.

Moira I don't know.

Stuart What does your contract say?

Moira I've never had a formal contract.

Stuart You can't just drive off in a camper van leaving him in the lurch.

Moira Of course I can't.

Stuart And you'll have to train your replacement. There will be a period of handover. Induction.

Moira Yes.

Stuart It'll be hard to replace you after all this time. Quite a wrench.

Roy We need another bottle opening. Any requests?

Moira I can think of a couple of requests that aren't anything to do with wine.

Roy I expect we all can. Italian? (*Begins to open the fourth bottle.*)

Stuart I'm already feeling jealous of you two in a camper van. To be able to . . . to feel brave enough to set off into the unknown –

Roy Wherever it is will be clearly marked on a map.

    Exit Moira, to inside.

Stuart Well, wherever it is, known or unknown, there you'll be. Somewhere new and unfamiliar. In a camper van together.

    Roy pulls the cork.

The open road, etcetera.

    Roy puts down everything. Exit Roy, to outside.

    End of Act One.

Act Two

Sian and Stuart look out towards the dark sea. There's a series of pounding waves, then voices carried on the wind, then quiet again.

Stuart She didn't know about the camper van.

Sian You said she didn't.

Stuart No, I said I didn't think he'd told her.

Sian 'Who was that family at the end of Stone Road?' You know full well who it was –

> *Stuart peers out through a window that's not in the direction of the sea. This window looks out towards Dr Godsave's home.*

Stuart And got hardly a flicker from either of them.

Sian And those crass suggestions about Dr Godsave?

Stuart He's home now. There's a light on. Those were perfectly innocent questions.

Sian Bollocks, were they.

Stuart If you think they were suggestive then they must have suggested something to you.

Sian How's Sue?

Stuart How's Ben?

Sian Where are Sue and Little Charlie, today?

Stuart At home.

> *Beats.*

Sian Grief is very powerful, isn't it? I'm having to be quite vigilant.

Stuart Vigilant?

Sian Monitoring my responses.

Stuart That'll be how you talk at work.

Sian Why are you goading Mum and Dad?

Stuart Goading them to what?

Sian I don't know.

Silence.

Stuart I'd love to know what someone else thinks. To think with someone else's brains. To be Mum, or Dad, for instance. Why do you think they had another child sixteen years after me?

Sian Why don't you ask them?

Stuart I heard Mum call Dr Godsave Philip this afternoon.

Sian That's his name, isn't it? Have you ever heard anyone else speculate about Mum and Dr Godsave or Dad and Janey Hudson?

Stuart Oh yeah, several people have stopped me in the street to say, 'Your mum and the doctor, eh? Your dad and that dead bird.'

Sian Be very careful, Stuart. Grief can open the door onto all sorts of reckless emotions. We're all in a very new, strange and powerful mode of being –

Stuart You mean we're all crazy. You can vigilantly monitor your responses to your new and strangely powerful mode of being and the rest of us will just get on with being fucking crazy and –

Enter Roy, carrying dirty plates, etc., which he adds to the piles. Pours himself some red wine.

24

Roy We shan't do camper van all the time, perhaps. But the weather's always good somewhere, if we're prepared to leave Europe. Just keep moving to where the sun is. Follow the sun. No bad weather. No cold weather, anyway. You can easily keep in touch; e-mails, e-pictures, e-text. Generator in the van, start it up, plug ourselves in, away we go. Mobile phones with international roaming. No problem.

Stuart Will you have separate bedrooms in this camper van?

Sian deliberately spills wine over Stuart.

Roy What was that?

Sian Sorry, sorry. So sorry.

Stuart (*hissed*) That was a legitimate question.

Sian (*hissed*) And that was a legitimate accident.

Roy You spilled some wine.

Stuart 'S all right, the suit needed cleaning anyway.

Roy I'm not worried about the suit.

Enter Moira, carrying nothing. She doesn't sit. Beats.

Stuart I went to see a financial adviser. He smiled as if remembering old lovers as he related the virtues of level-term assurance, pensions with profits, ISAs and trackers, and gilt-edged stakes. I said to him these all sounded sound investments, but I hadn't any money. His smile faded. He became exasperated, demanding to know why I'd come to see him. I said I was a fully qualified professional with eight years' experience, a wife, an infant child, but only a one-bed flat, because my profession is that of teacher. I'd come to see him – a financial adviser – to seek his advice on how to acquire some finance, above and beyond my paltry salary: extra finance to invest. I added that as and when I had successfully followed his advice in acquiring this extra finance, I would then be asking him his further advice on investing it.

Beats. Sian takes charge, slightly manically.

Sian A piece of paper each. A pen.

Stuart What for?

Sian A game?

Moira A game, today?

Sian A word game. The animals game, I suppose it could be called. Just a silly game. A break from it all. Vince said to me – the third time they said he had a few days to live – he said, 'At my funeral, get pissed and have a laugh.' So here goes. Three pens, three pieces of paper.

Stuart What about you?

Sian I know the game. Once you know it you can't play it.

Stuart Then it sounds like it might be a trick.

Sian It's a game.

Stuart I'm getting a bad feeling.

Sian Trust me, I love you. Trust me if you love me.

Stuart Gimme some wine.

Sian Not drunk enough to love me, yet? Here we go, then. Take up the pen and write down the meaning of life.

Roy Eh?

Sian Write it down.

Roy Eh?

Sian If you think that 'Eh?' is the meaning of life –

Moira (*to Sian*) He's having you on.

Roy (*about Sian*) She's having us on.

Sian Divide your paper up into sections.

Roy Columns?

Sian No, across.

Moira Like that?

Sian Yes. Three boxes. Yes. Right. Start in the middle box. Write the name of your favourite animal. Now three words that describe the qualities you admire, that this animal possesses. Three words. Associations – whatever comes to mind. Okay? Now, in the top section or box, write the name of your second favourite animal. Dad, I didn't mean to but I just caught a glimpse. Dad, you're writing a name.

Roy The name of the animal.

Sian I meant the species, not an actual name.

Roy You didn't say a species. You said the name of your favourite animal –

Stuart (*reading*) Skippy?

Roy So, I'm stupid.

Sian No one's accusing you of being stupid.

Roy I feel stupid.

Stuart (*to Moira*) And just to be helpful he's added in brackets 'the bush kangaroo'.

Roy Not everyone knows who Skippy is.

Stuart What's your first animal?

Roy It's wrong as well.

Stuart What is it?

Roy It doesn't matter. There. Crossed out.

Sian Okay –

Roy Obliterated. Stupid Dad.

Sian Okay –

Roy What an idiot. What a twat –

Moira Excuse me –

Sian Okay. We'll just give Dad some time to himself with a fresh piece of paper.

Moira Three sections across.

Roy I know.

Moira Middle box: favourite animal and three word associations –

Roy I know, Moira. Believe me, Moira, I know.

Moira Okay.

Roy Okay.

Sian Okay?

Roy Done.

Sian Okay. And then, in the bottom box –

Moira Third favourite animal?

Stuart Clever Mum.

Sian Etcetera, etcetera. Everyone done? Done?

Stuart No doubt we are being.

Sian Okay, and hand them over.

Roy I'm sorry, everyone.

Sian 'S okay. 'S only a game.

Moira Do our answers amuse you?

Sian Now, I've sat where you are sitting, believe me –

Stuart I don't like it, I don't like it.

Sian I'm going to read these out.

Stuart I don't like it.

Sian What you've written is a code. A code for your attitudes to sex. What the answers reveal is your attitudes before, during and after sex.

Stuart Fantastic!

Roy Oh no. Oh no.

Stuart What a fantastic game!

Sian No papers are returnable so you can take your hand back.

Roy I want mine.

Moira Treat it as the silly joke it obviously is.

Roy Not at my expense.

Moira Stuart likes questions and Sian likes games.

Sian I did it.

Roy Not with your mother and father and brother.

Sian Ben taught me it.

Roy If you insist on reading any of them out, I'll leave.

Stuart Out of all the people I have ever known, only you, Sian, could offer 'the animals game' as a laugh after the funeral of –

Roy Give them back!

Silence.

Moira Don't read them, Sian. Just give them back.

Sian Okay. (*Returns the papers.*)

Moira You take things too far. Think why we're here.
Lapse in taste, Sian. Poor taste.

Sian You all want to know what each other wrote,
though, don't you?

Moira You've never known when to stop. You've always
taken things too far.

Sian If I've never known when to stop, if I've always
taken things too far, that means I've always, since my birth,
gone too far, which suggests that if it wasn't behaviour
learned from you then it was a genetic instruction and,
as far as I am aware, there is no quest by members of the
scientific community to isolate the gene that causes
myself or anyone else to take things too far.

Moira Gobbledegook. All that gobbledegook is a perfect
example of you going off the rails and going too far.

Sian Off the rails as well, now?

Roy Your mother just means you're being your adorable
eccentric self.

Sian Okay. It wasn't a laugh. It might have been, but it
wasn't. But I still maintain that you all want to know
what each other wrote.

*Beats. The fourth bottle of red wine is nearly empty.
Sian drains it.*

Stuart Another bottle, methinks. Another bottle? Shall I
choose the next one? Why not? What does anyone think
of these plastic corks? Are they still called corks? I used
to think of winemaking as a rustic, primitive art: the bark

of a tree fashioned and thrust into the neck of the bottle by the hairy hand of a peasant. These plastics have no character at all.

Roy They do the job.

Stuart And is it called a plastic? And is that tool a plastic-screw? No, this is still a cork, and this is still a corkscrew.

Moira Are you still seeing someone yourself?

Sian No, no therapist, no counselling, no psychiatry, psychotherapy, analysis, shrinkage, talking it out, talking cure. I'm clean. I'm going straight. I just do other people. I'm in recovery, or, at least, in remission. No pills, either.

Moira You haven't taken any pills to induce your behaviour? Have a few of mine to calm you down.

Sian I've taken Valium in my time. I found it disagreeable.

Stuart What did people do with their time and money before Personal Development and Integral Yoga and Mentoring the Magical Child Within and Reiki and Feng Shui and Primal Integration and Crystal Healing?

Roy I had acupuncture when I was small. My mother took me. Chinese man down the road.

Sian Acupuncture – ancient discipline. What did the Chinese acupuncturist do?

Roy Stuck pins in me.

Sian Are you laughing at me, Stuart? What was your complaint?

Roy They hurt.

Sian Stuart, you are laughing at me, but let me tell you that I believe in the efficacy of all those therapies you listed and I'll tell you something else. I make shedloads of money out of them. Twice, three times what a teacher

31

earns. Are you laughing now? Good. Now, Dad. What was your illness?

Roy I wasn't ill, I couldn't sleep. Couple of hours a night. Odd naps here and there. I looked like shit. Excuse me, but there's no other word for it. Everything was tried. Eventually: acupuncture. Mother said we were going to a Chinese doctor. I'd never seen a real Chinese man. I was expecting a bloke with a ponytail, Fu Manchu moustache, wispy beard; a pagoda with a sampan parked outside. We went to an ordinary house and he was an ordinary Chinese man. Mother said, 'This is Roy,' and he led us into a room full of jars of things. And burning things. Smoke. He studied my tongue, held my wrists and he contemplated me.

Sian How old were you?

Roy Twelve. Or so. He put pins in the back of my hand and then, without warning, one right in the top of my head.

Stuart In your head?

Roy Right here. Right there, right in the middle.

Stuart Without warning?

Roy If he'd warned me I wouldn't have let him do it.

Stuart Sounds like acupuncture comes from the same school of pain as 'Deep-Tissue Therapy'.

Sian Did it work?

Roy Seemed to alleviate it for a while.

Sian What was the cause of the insomnia?

Roy I don't know.

Sian Insomnia can be hereditary.

Stuart I've never had it.

Sian I have piles of books by my bed. I listen to the World Service. We were never meant to sleep all night. Not eight hours straight through. Before the Industrial Revolution it was normal to have a break from sleep in the middle of the night. Have a snack. Chat. Even have sex, apparently. It was the demands of the factories, the demands of the industrio-capitalist complex, that created the modern pattern of sleep. I learnt that little tidbit in the middle of the night when I should have been asleep. (*Draws the cork on the fifth bottle of red wine.*) Actually, deep-tissue massage isn't my latest thing. My most recent thing is I've decided to try and treat everyone as if I'll never see them again.

Roy Jesus, Sian.

Sian What, Dad? It's my version of making everyone feel special. You know how they say of somebody, 'They made me feel like I was the only person in the room?' Well, my version of that is, 'She made me feel like she'd never see me again.' I admit it can unnerve some people. It can get a bit weird. A bit stripped naked. I try to really concentrate hard on each person. For instance, in a café when ordering 'a decaffeinated cappuccino with skimmed milk and a lo-fat muffin, please', I make eye contact. Really wanting them to know that I know that they exist.

Stuart And you wanting them to know that you exist.

Sian Yes, why not? A mutual recognition. Time, take a bit of time with your fellow human beings. Taking time actually takes no more time than rushing. Taking time can in fact save time. And I do the same in the sandwich bar at lunchtime. And when I'm buying a Travelcard in the newsagent's.

Moira Do you really go around all day worried that you'll never see people again?

33

Sian I mean 'see' as in 'know'. Who are you? Mum, Dad, brother. What do I know about you? Let's play another game, let's write down what we know about each other.

Stuart I don't want to play another game until we've finished the animals. Let me read them out.

Exit Roy to inside. Sian takes the animal answers from Stuart. Moira moves away to the outside door but doesn't exit. Beats. Sian crosses to Moira. Stuart moves to within earshot.

Sian (*to Moira*) I think we need a locutorium.

Moira A what?

Sian Monks in a silent order have a room called a locutorium. It's where they go to talk. At work I've designated a certain time in a certain room 'The Locutorium' –

Moira breaks away, pours herself a glass of wine, and exits to outside, remaining in view.

Stuart Nice try.

Sian At what?

Stuart Getting them to talk.

Sian I don't know what you mean.

Beats. Stuart can't work out if she's being straight.

Stuart Yeah, right. If Ben taught you that game, does that mean you're back together again?

Sian Why?

Stuart Talking about sex with him, weren't you?

Sian No, not back together again.

Stuart Is he seeing anyone else?

34

Sian Possibly. We deny our desire and it increases; we succumb to our desire and satisfaction is fleeting. We desire, we consume, we sadden.

Stuart You don't sound like you're talking as yourself, as if you're being yourself. You sound as if you're talking about a third person. I think the old Sian is sitting in front of me, then I find I've lost you again because you sound like one of those little self-help books full of homilies. The *Little Book* of that, the *Little Book* of this. You could write *The Little Book of Psychobollocks*.

Sian You should try some therapies.

Stuart If all these therapies are so great, how come you're still tangled with Ben?

Sian Can I ask – did you and Sue mean to conceive Little Charlie?

Stuart What?

Sian What's up? What's the matter? It's just talk. You want to know if Mum and Dad meant to conceive Vince.

Stuart Charlie was an accident. We didn't say beforehand, we didn't agree before the sexual intercourse we think it was that led to him: 'Let's try for a baby.' I do have to say, though, that if it was the particular shag we think it was, it was a humdinger that deserved a result.

Brother and sister see who will blink first.

(*suddenly angry*) Fucking Vince, fucking dying . . . He never smoked or did anything bad. Vegetarian from the age of four. It's mad, it's mad –

Sian I tried every therapy on him, every diet, every spell, even.

Stuart It's incomprehensibly unjust. And I'm unable to get drunk enough. Vince loved Little Charlie. And vice versa. Vince would have been a great dad when the time came. (*Beats.*) To change the subject slightly, Sian.

Sian Yes, Stuart, go ahead.

Stuart In your professional opinion, if you were therapising yourself, is your unhappiness ossified?

Sian My unhappiness?

Stuart Yes, your unhappiness. Isn't that what you're trying to cure? But, despite all your therapyisations, you can't –

Sian I don't consider myself to be unusually unhappy. I wouldn't claim unadulterated happiness, but I'm not overwhelmingly unhappy.

Stuart I am. I'm seriously unhappy with quite a lot of my impecunious life, as it happens.

Enter Moira, with empty glass.

You hear rich people say money can't buy you happiness, but I'd be willing to give it an effing try. When poor people like me hear rich people complaining that their money hasn't bought them happiness, we think, give me your money, then; I'll give it a darned sight better shot at being happy than you have. (*to Sian*) You're not rich, by the way, are you?

Moira You're not poor.

Stuart I'm not exactly affluent, either.

Moira (*to Sian*) And you'll find someone.

Sian Someone? Someone? Excuse me? Is it 'pity single Sian time' again? Please don't pity me. I don't mind being single. I can do what I like. And I do do it, quite often.

Moira I think it's a crime that you two can't remember being happy babies.

36

Sian Can you remember that?

Moira Me?

Sian Yes, you?

Moira Me remember you – of course.

Sian No, do you remember yourself?

Moira No.

Sian Then why should we?

Enter Roy from inside, carrying dirty plates, etc.,
which he adds to the piles. Pours himself a red wine.

Stuart We could all try 'rebirthing', perhaps. Is rebirthing
the correct term for –

Moira I'm trying to be serious, Stuart.

Stuart Danger! Danger! Mum being serious!

Moira You were all little and so plump and soft and
strong and ready and happy –

Sian Innocence, you're talking about innocence. True
innocence. Innocent bliss –

Moira You were both gurgling, fat things. That must be
somewhere in you –

Sian And in you, Mum. It is a crime, isn't it? To lose the
memory when 'Food please, warm please, love please,'
were all we desired –

Roy Isn't it a bit much – I mean, aren't you asking for
the impossible, over a certain age, to realistically expect
to experience innocent bliss?

Moira I wished you'd stayed happy babies. When you've
been horrible I've tried to remember you as happy babies –

Sian Were we all happy? Were we all equally happy?

Roy You talked earliest, and you've never shut up since –

Sian Do I talk more than Stuart? I don't think so –

Roy I thought what you did was called the listening cure?

Sian When you were hovering over us, what were you trying to preserve? Please tell me. Please.

    Beats.

Roy I was thinking of protecting you.

Stuart From what?

Roy The world. Things out there. (*to Stuart*) Done it?

Stuart Done what?

Roy Read them out?

Stuart No.

Roy Is he telling the truth?

Sian Yes.

    Roy clams up again. Beats.

Stuart The animals I chose in Crazy Sian's Fantastic Game were: favourite – dolphin; second favourite – leopard; third favourite – pepsis wasp. So, before sex, according to Sian's interpretation, I'm a leopard, and like a leopard I'm graceful, poised and exciting. During sex I'm an agile, playful and fast dolphin. After sex, I'm a pepsis wasp; surprising, immutable and cruel.

Roy I've never come across a pepsis wasp.

Moira Just as well, by the sounds of it.

Stuart By day it flies, a beautiful, winged creature. But at night it walks, stalks, searching for tarantula spiders in their holes. When it finds a tarantula hole it draws the

38

tarantula out and after a short skirmish, paralyses it with a sting. Then the pepsis wasp lays its eggs in the tarantula. Then the pepsis wasp pushes the tarantula back into its hole, paralysed but alive. The eggs hatch inside the paralysed tarantula. The baby pepsis wasps are born in their first dinner.

Roy How big is this wasp?

Stuart Big, for a wasp. It's a big motherfucker.

Moira Stuart!

Roy Yes, Stuart.

Stuart I will not accept any sort of reprimand from the man who said his favourite animal was Skippy the bush kangaroo. What animal did Skippy beat into second place?

Roy Moby Dick.

Stuart Shouldn't that be 'Moby Dick the white whale?'

Roy The same.

Sian There was a picture of him in one of our encyclopaedias –

Roy Yes, him leaping. He'd been pursued, and pursued, and attacked, and finally he'd turned, and instead of ramming the harpoon boats, he dived, disappeared, and the sea, frothing but a minute ago, became calm. Then he leapt, shot out of the water over by the main ship, he hung in the air over the main ship –

Sian The *Pequod* –

Roy He'd crept up – if whales can creep – on the *Pequod*, and the picture in your encyclopaedia caught him suspended at the very zenith of his leap, poised above the ship and its hapless mariners.

39

Beats.

Stuart Funny that the word 'dick' arises in a game about sex.

Beats. They look out to sea. Quiet waves lap the seashore.

Sian What was the last thing Vince said?

Roy We were both out of the room.

Moira Apparently he didn't really say anything.

Sian The last question he asked me was about your sleeping arrangements at Auntie Pat's. I told him you were sharing a room, that either Auntie Pat was unaware of your domestic arrangements or she was ignoring them. Auntie Pat wasn't pressed for space, was she? There were empty bedrooms.

Roy Full stop. End of story.

Sian What's that?

Roy Drink some more. Relax. And you, Stuart. Tell us about how good your life is. Tell us about you and Sue and Little Charlie. We'll have to stop calling him little. He won't be little for very much longer, unless there's a problem. Soon, he'll be able to interrogate you and Sue.

Stuart Morning. Breakfast. Our places laid on the dining-room table. Dad's place laid in here. Laid the night before. Cereal bowl, cup, saucer, place mat, napkin, spoons, glass for fruit juice, paperback book. Airport novels. Did you only read those books at breakfast?

Moira You make it sound like a cruel ritual when in fact your father couldn't cope with you first thing –

Stuart I stopped bringing friends home. 'This is Mum's bedroom. This is Dad's.' . . . 'No, I don't know why. Why do you ask?' . . . 'What's not normal?' . . . 'Your parents sleep together?!' Did you have a row? And are you still having it? Is either of you gay, perhaps?

Roy 'If that's what you think, what can we say? Full stop. End of story.'

Stuart What's that?

Moira I'm not a lesbian.

Roy And neither am I.

Stuart Does separate bedrooms mean separate sex?

Moira This subject is not your business.

Stuart I'm fascinated by you.

Sian And I'd quite like to know.

Stuart You are our parents . . . You know about our lives . . . When we were happy babies –

Roy Too many people tell everything about themselves! Smirking confessions about reprehensible actions – no real shame, or guilt, or morality. I've seen them on TV. Why are the televisions in hospital waiting rooms always tuned to remorseless dross? Human beings feigning regret, mimicking remorse. 'I can't help it, I don't know why I do it, it's just me, it's just the way I am. I don't know why I joyride/burgle/mug/shoplift/dole-cheat/ have three children by three different women and don't provide for any of them/sleep with my boyfriend's friends.' Would you two rather you came from a broken home? Would that explain your failures?

Stuart Which failures?

Roy You know what I mean.

Stuart Nearly everything about me, I expect.

Roy And then there's your sister's never-ending miserable on-off saga with that Ben –

Sian I still see Ben.

Roy Of course you do, now and again. When either of you fancy it, when one of you can be bothered? An 'open' relationship, is it? You don't know you've been born –

Stuart What does that phrase mean? Where does it come from?

Roy Who cares?

Stuart I care, because it's crap. We all know we've been born, it's patently obvious, so to say you don't know is ridiculous.

Roy We've a daughter who says she's treating people as if she might never see them again and a son who's acting as if he doesn't care if he never sees us again.

Stuart What's that? Is that a threat? You'll be off in your van, anyhow. When Mum gets it together to resign.

Roy 'Full stop. End of story.' I mean it.

He exits, to outside. Moira drifts to the window that looks out at Dr Godsave's. Sian fixes her attention deliberately on her mother.

Moira We've all drunk too much.

Sian Truth's lubricant. Tell us things.

Stuart We want blood, and you and Dad are the stones.

Sian Offer things, and we'll offer things.

Moira Such as?

Sian Truths.

A moment between Moira and Sian.

Stuart (*butting in*) 'Full stop, end of story': where's Dad's new refrain come from?

Moira (*looking at Sian*) Daytime TV.

Enter Roy from outside with dusty gizmo. (The gizmo is a home-made toy that consists of a wire along which you try to pass a metal loop without touching the wire. If you do touch it, a buzzer sounds.)

Roy What about if we play a proper game? If you can get further than me, we'll have to answer questions –

Moira We'll? You'll.

Sian We're all too pissed for gizmo.

Roy Level playing field, then.

Stuart That's another stupid expression. Why does a playing field have to be level?

Roy So it's fair.

Stuart Tell me a game where the teams don't change ends at half-time; tell me a game where only one team has to battle the inequalities of the terrain –

Roy gets gizmo to buzz.

Roy Heads or tails?

Sian Tails.

Roy I win. You go first.

Sian gets quite a long way. Roy burps to try to distract her. Sian stops and stares at him. Roy smiles at her.
Sian resumes gizmo. It buzzes at three-quarters of the way.
Roy's turn. He's going well. Halfway along he stops, smiles at Sian and sings:'I'm a Yankee doodle dandy, Yankee doodle do or die,' etc., before resuming. As he's reaching the point Sian achieved:

Moira There's not a cat in hell's chance that I'll ever go away in a sodding camper van.

The buzzer buzzes.

Roy Bloody hell. Shit.

Moira I didn't want to put you off. It just came out. I'm sorry. I didn't mean to put you off. You should have another go.

Roy The challenge is void.

Stuart It's what?

Roy I'm declaring it void.

Stuart You can have another go.

Roy Not fair.

Stuart Not fair if you don't.

Roy Not fair if I do.

Stuart Okay, go again. Both go again.

Roy No. Game over.

Stuart Sian was going to win.

Roy I think I was.

Stuart If you're so sure, go again.

Roy No.

Stuart This is cheating!

Roy How is it? Mum put me off. The game is void.

Exit Roy to outside, with gizmo.

Sian Boys, boys, boys, boys, boys.

Exit Stuart, to inside. Beats. The women contemplate the dark sea and the dark horizon. A dog barks in the distance.

Moira I like Ben. He's been around a long time.

Sian You were cruel to Ben.

Moira To Ben? I was? To Ben?

Sian And to me. And to yourself.

Moira Me? I was?

Sian When Vince was given a week to live. The first time, the first time they said he might die within days, over a year ago, when Ben was on retreat in Spain, the day before I was going out to join him I had to ring him to say Vince would die within days, and Ben flew back. He gave up his retreat halfway through and came to stay with us at Auntie Pat's, and Ben was great, just great to have around because the tension was, it was just . . . unbearable. What with Vince dying and you and Dad sharing a bedroom. Did you share the bed? What did you do?

Moira is inscrutable.

And after three days of Ben being there we were all in the car, driving away from the hospital, and you and Dad must've had a conversation with the consultant because you turned – no, you didn't turn, you did it via the mirror, you looked at us in the mirror, and you said to Ben that it now looked as if it was a false alarm, that Vince wasn't expected to die imminently, he'd rallied, so Ben could go back and resume his retreat.

Moira What's cruel about that?

Sian You told him to go.

Moira He could retreat to his retreat, cross his little legs, and hum himself silly.

Sian You didn't tell him to go for his benefit. You didn't want him to stay.

Moira There was no need for him to stay.

Sian Why didn't you explain that Vince was in remission, and ask what Ben wanted to do?

Moira Then he'd feel guilty if he chose to go.

Sian I think you told him to go because you couldn't stand him being around because he and me were in stark relief to you and Dad.

Moira No –

Sian Me and Ben reminded you of what you and Dad weren't.

Moira No.

Sian You wanted me to be as unhappy as you –

Moira We should have all been – what, larking about?

Sian No, trying to live. Just being alive for moments – just flashes of light in the gloom. Just being silly for a moment. Like when earlier we were guessing the country of origin of the wine – a silly game, you knock your glass over but don't acknowledge it in the normal way. It's like a poltergeist has visited. You act like a poltergeist –

Moira I heard you laugh, young madam, I heard you laugh!

Sian You heard me what?

Enter Roy, from outside.

Moira I heard you laugh when Ben was there. You and Ben were in a room at Auntie Pat's and you were heard laughing!

Sian A room? What room?

Moira Your room.

Sian Our bedroom?

46

Moira Your room at Auntie Pat's.

Sian Mine and Ben's bedroom at Auntie Pat's? You were listening at the door?

Moira No, I wasn't listening at your door, it was a loud laugh. Like this. (*Laughs.*) One loud laugh. One full laugh.

Sian How selfish. How cruel. How cruel to laugh. How selfish to laugh. You wrote to the Archbishop of Canterbury about Vince, didn't you?

    Moira tries to stare Sian down. Enter Stuart from inside, carrying dirty plates, etc.

Moira I think I might have.

Sian Didn't do any good. If I laughed it was because Ben was teaching me the animals game. He'd developed it on retreat, intending to incorporate it in his new diploma: 'Animal Archetypes in the Psycho-Sexual Drama of the Self'. What's funny? What's making you smile? It's a proper course. It's accredited by . . . Look. There. I almost went. Almost lost my composure, just as you regained yours. Isn't that a coincidence, Mother?

Moira Here we go. Blame everyone but yourself.

Sian Blame everyone for what?

Moira The state of your life.

Sian What state?

Moira It doesn't matter.

Sian No, go on.

Moira It doesn't matter.

Sian Yes, it does.

Moira Have a child.

Roy Moira –

Moira If you had a child you'd have something positive to focus on. You'd stop thinking about yourself all the time. Your body and your mind are demanding a child. Your soul demands it.

Sian Should I go it alone – go to an agency for some sperm? Or should I have this child with Ben, whom you claim to like?

Moira I don't know; I don't know how things are organised these days. You and Ben aren't a couple in the normal sense, I know, but your relationship endures, which is something.

Sian A child, a child would solve everything, would it? But with Ben? I don't know. We're 'off' at the moment. I'm trying to end it. Finally. For ever. Because the last time we were 'on', and I moved in again, after the initial euphoria, it was terrible, again. I moved out. Blah blah blah. I moved out, I called him to meet for a civilised discussion about ending it for ever, with the possibility of remaining friends. We meet and I ask for my stuff back, and he says what stuff, and I say the stuff I brought with me and the stuff I paid for, like the microwave.

And he says that microwave broke and he'd had to buy a new microwave and I say how did it break and he says it wore out and I say I didn't wear it out and he agrees that of course I didn't, it finally wore out after I'd left, but some of the wear must have happened whilst I was there and I say where does that leave me, then?

And he says, well, you can't have my new microwave if that's what you're thinking, I paid for that, and I say, what else got broken, what about all my other kitchen stuff?

And he says it's around somewhere and I say did you check the list I sent you and he says that I'm looking well

48

and what now? And I say what do you mean, what now?
And he says is it really the stuff that you want from me,
and I say the stuff is all I want from you, and he asks if
I'm seeing anyone and I say can we concentrate on the
stuff and he asks again are you seeing someone and I say
if it's any of your business, no, I'm not, I'm single – for
want of a better word – and he says I didn't mean are you
with a bloke I meant are you seeing any kind of healer?

And I say I don't need therapy and he says he didn't
say therapist he said healer, which we all need one of, we
all do, anyone who's had parents anyone who's alive is
damaged and needs healing, needs therapy, and I say is
that whose fault it is, then, and he says not their fault.

Not their fault.

And I say I'm not mad, it's you, if either of us is mad it
is you. You, Ben, want me to be mad, men have always
insinuated women are mad when they are disobedient,
and he says you aren't disobeying me, I haven't issued
any orders and who was it introduced the word 'mad'
into this conversation – not me. And he says he'd like to
be friends and I say we'll see and he asks when I'd like to
pick up the stuff and I say I'm not going to pick it up,
someone else will pick it up, I'll pay someone, that would
be healthier, and he says look, I don't want you any
more, not like that, and he says I was right to leave and it
was right for him, too, and he says the bed, that isn't
worn out, and I feel a lurch in my gut and I say good.

And he says we bought that bed together, and I say I
paid for it, you had no money, I paid for it and you never
gave me the half you promised and he says that was our
bed, we held a ceremony to bless it, and I say it's just a
bed and I've got to go now and he says remember the
good times and I say I try to and he says can I kiss you
and I say yes, on the cheek.

And he says he has good memories and I say so do
I and he says you do? And I say I'd be pretty stupid to

have loved him on and off all these years if I hadn't enjoyed some of it and we part. And I don't pay someone else, I borrow a van . . . and phone him . . . and he says yes, that's fine, that time . . . and I go round and a female answers the door. He's got a woman there and she doesn't know who I am or that I was coming around for my stuff, and –

Roy Come here. Come here, come here, come here. Come here. Let me hold you. Come. Come. Let me.

Sian (*to Roy*) You used to come into my room and give me money and you had tears in your eyes. You'd give me a fiver or a tenner and say that it was the best thing you could give me and you had tears in your eyes.

Roy I'm sorry.

Sian It's not Ben's fault. It's the combination of us. That female who answered the door – she doesn't know she's a pawn in the great game called Sian and Ben. But I'm never living with Ben ever again and I'm never sharing possessions again and I'm never having a child.

Moira When you find someone you can trust you'll forget you said that.

Sian No, I won't.

Moira You'll want to share things with them.

Sian I want to share things with Ben. He's the love of my life and if I don't get to the bottom . . . if I don't crack me and Ben, I'll never crack anything. I just want you to be happy. I just want my parents to be happy. (*to Moira and Roy*) I just want you to do what you want to do, whatever that is.

Exits to outside. Moira and Roy avoid each other's eyes.

Roy Leave her. She'll be all right.

Stuart Ben that, Ben this. He's got some sort of hold over her.

Moira He's charismatic. He's very likeable.

Stuart He abuses his power. He's a quack.

Roy Ain't that the truth? 'Full stop. End of story.'

Stuart What is this phrase you've acquired –

Roy Fancy a Scotch?

Stuart – this vocal tic uttered in strange voices?

Roy Daytime TV. There was a young bloke and two young women, both with children by him. (*Pours Scotch.*) He shuttled between the families, living off both, providing for neither. Both women thought he was finished with the other. I can't remember his name. Let's call him Jez. Or Wez. Or Bez.

> *Exit Moira to inside.*

The first woman claimed Jez or Bez or Wez had had sex with her the night before the programme, whilst the second woman said he'd told her that he hadn't had sex with the first woman for over a year. The first woman revealed that last night wasn't a one-off: 'We do it every week when he comes round to see Ricky' – or Bicky or Wicky or Sicky – whatever her poor child's name was. The women tried to prove that the other was lying, but it was Jez, Bez or Wez who was the biggest liar, of course. The audience turned on him, and whenever one of the women, or the host, or a member of the live studio audience picked Jez, Bez or Wez up on something he said that was obviously untrue he'd utter the refrain: 'If that's what you think, what can I say? Full stop. End of story.'

The women tried to get at each other – physically. Jez or Bez or Wez shrugged as if to say, 'Look at what they're like,' and at the end of the show both women wanted

him to live with them and them alone. Beyond help. If
women are obviously prepared to accept so little, why
should men improve?

Beats. Looks, looks away.

Stuart But at least they've been on the telly –

Roy People these days think they have a right to be
happy. They think everything's their right. Citizens'
rights, human rights –

Stuart You never cried when you came to my room to
give me money.

Roy Your sister's exaggerating.

Stuart You weren't crying, then?

Roy Once, perhaps.

Stuart I laughed like you the other day.

Roy Really?

Stuart Little Charlie fell over in a playground – he wasn't
hurt – and I laughed like you. (*ignoring Roy's baleful
glare*) Since Charlie's birth, Sue's been 'post-natally
depressed', you know.

Roy We thought there was something.

Stuart But you've never asked, have you?

Roy We were respecting your privacy.

Beats.

Stuart I had sex with a young mother. I was out on my
own, miserable. Drinking. Up in London. Met her, a
stranger, by Green Park. Got talking. Went into the park.
Fumbled. Groped. She was still lactating. Really turned
me on.

Roy Stop it.

Stuart Stop what?

Roy Turning yourself inside out.

Stuart I'm just talking.

Roy No, you're not. It's all selfish, all self-indulgent. The people on daytime TV confess and expect reward, they think they earn sympathy by admitting their pathetic ineptitudes. Daytime TV provides them with an audience that mirrors themselves, to whom they can parade their inadequacies. They don't offer their confessions as a cautionary tale or as an element of a redemptive story.

Stuart So Sue was at home depressed and there I was, screwing a woman who was herself still breast-feeding. And it was horny.

Roy Perhaps happiness for you has become confused with excitement.

Stuart You might be right, there. No, actually, it didn't turn me on sexually, it wasn't horny. I was determined to tell the truth about me and the lactating woman but somewhere along the line I began to dissemble, to veer away from painful shit that I'd like to sweep – I see you do this; you set off to tell the truth but then, somehow, you lose concentration. If you're like me – if I'm like you, you set out to be honest, but then you realise later that you haven't been. You realise there's been a gap, a sort of coma, between then, when you intended to be honest, and now, when you remember that you meant to be honest but you haven't been. So, what happened with the lactating woman was that we commenced sexual intercourse in Green Park and there was all this fluid soaking our upper parts and clothing, and it was only when I tasted the fluid and got a huge hit of memory that I realised it was breast milk coming from her. And thank

God the park was dark because I began weeping floods. Trails of tears from my eyes and thick rivulets of snot from my nostrils and racking sobs from somewhere, somewhere, some plunging depth, inside of me. Thank God we were having desperate sex because that's about the only activity that I'm aware of apart from prolonged torture with that elbow in the head thing of Sian's that could camouflage the feelings I was being overwhelmed by. Desperate sex with a female stranger . . . the scent and taste of her breast milk mixed in with the reek of sex . . . Not horny . . . The whole of my essential, human, animal self was briefly all connected and illuminated. I was fulfilled. Momentarily. Now, since, what would make me happy would be a good clear-out of everything. A really, really, total shit-out of everything.

Roy Of what?

Stuart A streamlining of my life. One me. One belief. One big thing to stick it all together. Or a quest. Some great purposeful adventure. A test. A discernible, physical test. Rites of passage with definite, dangerous obstacles to conquer. I'd like to survive near-death and be left clean. Stripped to basics. What's the thing that most scares you?

Roy You want me to talk about myself?

Stuart I dare you.

Roy Without slipping into lies?

Stuart Try not to. Fight against that. Concentrate . . . Okay, I'll ask you a question. The Hudsons who lived at the end of Stone Road; there's a rumour about you and –

Roy A rumour?

Beats. Stuart backs down.

What rumour? About whom, what? Spread by whom? I knew them. We used to pass each other, of course.

Given that we lived in the same road. There was eye contact. Hello's. Nothing was ever done, as such –

Stuart So there was something?

Roy Nothing real. I made up a silly fantasy. Like a child's imaginary friend. Leave fantasies as fantasy! Leave them! . . . In reality, nothing, but I feel her breath on my cheek. From time to time. I find that I've adopted her as my guardian angel. And as my bittersweet disappointment. My what-would-have-been-if-only. When I heard that she'd died at the time – when I heard the raw fact that she'd died and the ambulance was for her, I –

Stuart While that ambulance was still there you called me to come for a walk on the beach in the rain.

Roy I called you? I think you wanted to come.

Stuart You remember that clearly?

Roy Well, yes. You chased after me. I remember the ambulance, the rain, you.

Beats. Stuart seems to be wondering whether to challenge Roy.

Stuart Okay.

Roy Okay, what?

Stuart I'm not certain of my recollection, so I'm not disputing whether you called me or I chased after you.

Roy Whadya mean, disputing it?

Stuart Are you saying that you didn't call me?

Roy What is this about, Stuart?

Stuart I'm trying to get our stories to match, that's all. I'm trying to establish whether there's any consensus in our memories.

Roy It was just a walk on the beach. Perhaps you were called by me, perhaps you chased after me. It's possible I called you, because I don't remember categorically –

Stuart And you were upset because you'd just learned the body in the ambulance was Janey Hudson –

Roy Yes, I agree, I was probably upset and so were you, which makes it possible you chased after me, your father, because you were quite sensitive until the onset of puberty. Whereupon you became a sort of, a sort of howl of a boy; the red, sore, pustulated, suppurating, howling, youth you remained until you settled into your present incarnation. I say settled – you're not settled, are you?

Stuart We walked on the beach in the rain in silence. Just the squish of our feet in the wet sand until I noticed you weren't by me. You'd slipped me just like Little Charlie slips me sometimes. That terrible drop in the pit of the stomach and instant panic. I turned and found you thigh-deep in the waves, looking out to sea . . . I thought you might wade away; you'd walk into the horizon.

Roy I thought I saw something in the water.

Stuart Oh – what?

Roy A swimmer, a seal. You know – something in the swell.

Stuart Oh. I see.

Roy I walked out to get a better look. You cried 'Daddy! Daddy!' And I came back in.

Stuart You did.

Beats.

Since becoming the father of a son I'm almost psychically sensitive to newspaper stories about the tragic death of boys. Every newspaper I touch I can open to an article –

if there is one – about a boy who's gone adrift in a boat within sight of the shore, or boys who fall from boats whose fathers dive in after them and they're both lost. And then there's the father and his small son, digging lugworms on mudflats, caught by the combination of rising tide and sea mist. People can hear them shouting but can't see them for the mist, and can't locate them from their shouts because the mist distorts the sound. And the flats shift, anyway, so you can't trust them to be where they were. What people could tell was that the man and his son were shouting that the water was rising; that the boy was on his father's shoulders. Then there was just the boy's voice. I imagine the dad willing himself to grow taller so his boy –

Roy You can't imagine how it feels to lose a son.

Stuart No, I . . . Yes, I . . . No, not really.

Beats.

Roy I'm secretly terrified that your mother isn't going to come away in our Winnebago.

Stuart Winnebago, is it now? Well, perhaps she'll be more taken with the prospect of a Winnebago, if you ever get around to asking her properly.

Roy Perhaps if I'd said Winnebago from the off – if Winnebago was the first vehicle mentioned, she'd've been more receptive. Dr Godsave is everything I'm not. Did you see him today? Is there a man in your world who makes you feel that he's everything you're not? Godsave's a winning, wealthy, widower; whereas I'm a wasted, witless, wanker. I wonder what Dr Godsave's animals would be in Sian's game? When Vince was on his last legs, I tried hovering over him. I'm pissed, as usual. I feel old. My latest fantasy is that I'm in a crowd of strangers and a young woman takes to me and, overcoming my initial scepticism, I agree with her that I am the sexiest man in the world. And as we make love – vigorously, I might add – the crowd whoops and cheers and generally applauds.

Stuart Where is this crowd? Describe the locale.

Roy It starts on a pavement. A wide pavement in a town or city. The weather's spring-like. I can smell hot bread. I can hear mellow guitar music. The girl and I are making love against a window, a shop window, inside the shop, fabulous display –

Stuart She's a girl, now –

Roy Early twenties. A policeman – who's smiling – knocks on the glass and invites us up onto a stage in the street so that more people can see us, and we give each other a good seeing-to.

Stuart That's a pretty convincing would-be-alpha-male fantasy.

Roy Is the lactating woman a true story?

Stuart It isn't a story. It happened.

Roy I expect you haven't told Sue about it.

Stuart Have you ever told Mum about your fantasy affair with Janey Hudson?

Roy No. Can I ask you another something?

Stuart Go ahead.

Roy And you promise to tell the truth?

Stuart I'll try.

Roy Do you know anything I don't?

Stuart About what?

Roy About anything?

Stuart You'll have to be slightly more specific.

Roy Tonight, your mum, she's – it feels like she's doing something.

Stuart We've all been getting at each other. It's the way we've always been.

Roy No, you're 'getting at', Sian's delving and probing like a . . . and your mum's . . .

Stuart I think the thinking is, that as we're going through a shit time anyway, shit that might have been swept under the carpet is not being swept there. The carpet was lifted ready for the shit to be swept under it, but it hasn't been. And, moreover, as the carpet's been lifted and remains lifted, old shit has been uncovered, and is being addressed.

Roy Shit's being addressed?

Stuart The carpet's been lifted.

Roy Revealing shit?

Stuart Yes. Old shit.

Roy And we're addressing it?

Stuart Yes.

Beats.

Roy So, the carpet's been lifted and there's two piles of shit – one ready to be swept under, one already under.

Stuart Yes.

Roy I think I get the picture. We should start on those plates.

They don't.

Stuart D'ye think Sian will ever properly split from Ben the charismatic?

Roy I don't know. It doesn't feel like they do split up, because several times she's said they've split up and then later . . . So often, the cycle feels normal. Sian shouldn't announce it. I've never told anyone we've split up.

Stuart Hang on, are you saying that you and Mum have split up and not told anyone?

Roy I'm saying that in thirty years there's been several times I've split up with your mum and not told even her. And I'm sure she's done the same. How d'ye think our marriage has survived? We split up and then we try again without manifestly doing any of it. You lot are too impetuous. And you reveal too much – not enough guile.

Stuart May I inquire, then, what you believe is the present state of your marital affairs?

Roy Well, there's a couple of things irking me, but as I want her to join me in the Winnebago of my dreams I'll keep them to myself . . . But, but . . . We haven't turned to each other about Vince. We just haven't. We've got out of the habit. Our present habit is a bad habit.

Stuart I have another confession.

Roy Another woman?

Stuart No, a man.

Roy Not lactating, I hope.

Stuart I rang Dr Godsave to tell him to stop fucking with my family –

Roy You did what?

Stuart I said I rang –

Roy What did he say?

Stuart He said, 'This is Dr Godsave' –

Roy After you'd warned him off – what did he say after you'd . . . ?

Stuart Nothing.

Roy Nothing?

Stuart I rang him and he answered and he said, 'This is Dr Godsave, I'm afraid I can't come to the phone, but leave a mess –'

Roy It was his ansaphone?

Stuart Yes. He was still here, so he couldn't answer the phone at home.

Roy You rang him whilst he was still here?

Stuart 'Philip' was really pissing me off.

Roy And you left a message on his ansaphone saying 'Don't fuck with my family'?

Stuart No.

Roy But you said that you told him to stop fucking with your –

Stuart No, I rang him to tell him, and that's what I would have said if he'd answered in person, what I will say when I get to speak to him in person –

Roy But you knew he was here when you phoned him!

Stuart Don't get cross with me, I could have left a message, but I didn't, okay?

Roy You fucking idiot.

Stuart Fucking idiot your fucking self.

Roy I'm sorry. You're not an idiot. Not a fucking idiot.

Stuart Apology fucking accepted.

Roy Nothing's going on, you know?

Stuart No?

Roy No. But if you speak to him like that he'll know I think there is and that I am scared of him.

Stuart Dad, I'm going to ask you directly: did you have sexual relations with that woman, Janey Hudson?

Roy I did not.

Stuart So when you walked out into the sea after you discovered she'd died, that was not the desperate act of a forlorn lover?

Roy No . . . Stuart?

Stuart Yes?

Roy Did you really have sex with the lactating woman?

Stuart Yes. And ever since I've been deciding whether it's the end of my marriage and how that might affect Little Charlie. The lie that I've told Sue by not telling her the truth; it sits there, like a stone, between us.

Roy looks away because Stuart might break down.

End of Act Two.

Act Three

Another series of bigger waves. Roy and Stuart look out to sea. Voices on the wind.
Enter Sian from outside.

Sian I've been in the sea, paddling. It's cold, of course.

Stuart When is it warm?

Enter Moira from inside, carrying a small box.

Sian I love the sea here at night. One minute the waves are kissing your toes, the next they're looming out of the darkness, making you flee –

Moira We should go through these things together –

Sian I love it.

Exit Roy to inside.

Moira Let me know when you're ready.

Stuart Ready for what? Why d'ye talk to him like that? Do you know how you talk to him?

Sian and Stuart glance inside the box.

Sian When I said I'm treating people as if I'll never see them again that was the wrong way of describing what I'm doing. It's more accurate to say that I'm treating them as if they matter, as if they count, as if they're special. Vince taught me to do it. Every time we said goodbye. He had a gift. As I remember, I feel a rush of euphoria that I knew him. That we walked together for a while. *(to Moira)* Can I touch you?

Moira jerks away.

I'd like to touch you.

Moira moves away.

Please don't shrink away from me.

Beats.

Moira You can touch me, but no thumbs, no elbows.

Sian Let me stroke your face.

Moira lets her. It goes on for a while. Moira closes her eyes.

Since the first time I walked out on Ben –

Moira opens her eyes.

Please listen.

Beats. Moira closes her eyes.

Since the first time, I've learnt that because I walked out once, I'll walk out again; and in our case, again and again and again; because we've incorporated me walking out into the script of our relationship –

Moira looks at her through one eye.

Mum, you're going to have to let me use some jargon; it's the vocabulary I'm used to.

A beat. Moira closes her eye.

We know it'll happen – that I'll walk out when our relationship arrives at a certain juncture. We get there deliberately, sometimes. I can see the juncture coming three or so moves off and I'm mentally packing my bag. I know that Ben will do 'a'. And I'll feel 'b'. And he'll say 'c'. And there I'll go.

Moira He was living with someone when you met, wasn't he?

Sian Yes.

Moira You were very upset.

Sian Yes.

Moira Because he didn't tell you that he was living with someone until after you'd told him you loved him?

Sian I wanted him more, then. And he left her for me, and it was all very dramatic. That's what he thrives on. The drama. But he loves me the most because instead of our relationship ending for ever when he's caught having an affair, I walk. I walk off with our drama. He's left with his affair but I'm over there somewhere with our drama, distracting him. After a while we start an affair and he tells the other woman he's made a mistake.

Moira Who was the woman who you didn't know when you went round to get your stuff?

Sian Now, she's a worry. I didn't know of her existence. She's not the one I thought he was having an affair with when I walked out. This is a new thing. I don't think I'll be walking back in. She was pregnant –

Moira opens her eyes. Sian tries to continue speaking as if she's not upset.

I'll talk to him about it one day. Perhaps. He was always adamant he never wanted children. I told him it'd be all right, he could decide how involved he was, he'd still be able to do everything. He didn't have to live with us.

Stuart Perhaps Ben's understanding of your relationship – his affairs, your walks out and in – is that whatever he does, you'll come back.

Sian You're implying that he's getting what he wants but I'm not. No. Yes. No. You see, it's too late to have what I want with Ben. It was too late before the start. So I'm

65

settling for what I have, with Ben. He's great. He's exciting. I wish I'd just had an affair with him. He's great at affairs. Vince always asked about Ben. We had a shorthand. He'd ask: 'Off or on?' I use it as the title for my relationship workshop. I'm making a lot of money. I've been told I'm inspirational. I know you think I'm a mess and I'm sorry about the animals game. I get into situations and I can't get out of them. You're right, I do take things too far. But that's because I have the gift of spontaneity. I feel unhinged for a few minutes, then I get my balance back. Some of my clients envy me. They say I can access a state of wisdom. There's a celebrity psychiatrist agony-aunt who wants to pay me to be her constant psycho-spiritual guide. I'll pass some of the money on to you, Stuart. I don't need any, really. And Mum?

Moira Yes?

Sian What are you and Dad going to do now Vince has gone?

Beats. Unexpectedly, instead of becoming cross, Moira smiles to herself.

Moira He was conceived in here. We started on the draining board. Completely unexpected. We were so out of practice we fell off the draining board, finished up on the floor. It was at the time that you (*Stuart*) were sitting your A levels. You'd (*Sian*) already left home, and I was getting ready to leave.

That makes Stuart and Sian sit up.

I'd planned to leave after you two.

Stuart Why were you going to leave?

Moira Because I couldn't completely dispel the refrain that nagged in my head – the refrain that goes:, 'Is this it?' Because my spirit dreams, and drifts off, and I have to call it back.

Silence.

Stuart Does Dad know you were going to leave?

Moira He can't have known for certain, because I've never told anyone.

Stuart Were you going far away?

Moira I don't know.

Stuart Alone?

Moira Yes.

Sian Did you mean to get pregnant?

Moira No. Not consciously. I don't know.

Sian Did Dad mean you to?

Moira I don't know.

Sian What did you say when you found you were pregnant? How did he react?

Moira I told him I was pregnant. He said, 'Okay.'

Sian That's all?

Moira He smiled as he said it. Full stop, end of story. You think you can analyse, diagnose and generally second-guess us because you think that because you talk about everything emotional it somehow makes you wiser than us, but it doesn't.

Sian So one minute I should have a child because I'm too selfish and the next minute I think about other people too much? Which is it, Mother?

Moira Sian?

Sian Yes?

Moira Give up. This family's a mess and we always shall be. And you're part of the mess. A result and a cause of the mess.

Sian I refuse to jettison what I know in my soul to be true, but . . . Okay. Give me a minute. A few deep breaths. Okay. There we go. I have given up. I'm divorcing this family. I'll go to a solicitor – I'll go to America, I bet you can divorce your family there . . .

Moira and Stuart think she means it.

Joke!

Stuart You can understand why we weren't sure.

Moira And what about you, Stuart?

Stuart What about me?

Moira 'Back off' is the modern term for that which you should do, I think.

Stuart Okay.

Moira Okay. Now I'll tell you some other things. When Vince started dying, the consultant told me that your father privately offered all his organs that he could donate without actually dying himself. And later he privately offered the organs that would mean his own death. Not that your father's liver could be of any use to anyone. And today he was supposed to be reading a eulogy he'd privately written. The vicar told me.

Stuart Does Dad tell you anything himself?

Moira No, you have to work it out. For example, I caught him with a tear in his eye last year. He was reading the paper. I got it out of the bin later to see what it was that might have set him off. I think it was a piece about some men who fell into Surrey. Young Afghanis who'd stowed away in the wheel-housing of a jet bound for prosperous Europe. They froze to death, and when the wheel housing opened for landing, they fell out. Landed in Esher. Terrible. Still, you can't cry about every stranger, you'd be a stick, you'd be completely dehydrated. And you (*Sian*), you compass too much. We can't compass everyone. We can't be too naked, either. We can't be *écorché* –

Sian Can't be what?

Moira Hooray! Hooray! I know a word my daughter does not! Dr Godsave has an *écorché* figure in the surgery – a model of a human, flayed, stripped of skin. The opposite of thick-skinned. This family is crap. We're all crap. Give in, both of you. Go with it. I'm a crap mother. You're a crap daughter. You're a crap son. He's a crap father –

Stuart But a good husband. I think marriage is for life so I'm going to tell you in confidence that he didn't have an affair with Janey Hudson, not a real one –

> *Enter Roy from outside.*
> *If Stuart was a young child, Moira would ruffle his hair.*
> *Roy gestures the children to leave. They exit.*

Roy Did I say I'd eat breakfast alone?

Moira You picked up your plate one morning and came in here.

Roy And then?

Moira The next day you left the dining room again.

Roy I said I wanted to be alone here?

Moira We didn't really talk about it.

69

Roy You laid this table for me?

Moira After a while. You didn't comment on it so I assumed it was what you wanted.

Roy You seem to remember quite clearly what happened.

Moira Not in every detail.

Roy I feel at a disadvantage.

Moira I don't see why.

Roy The children seem to regard it as very significant that I ate breakfast separately.

Moira Oh well. File it under 'another thing we didn't talk about', along with why you started sleeping in another room.

Roy I had my insomnia. I didn't want to disturb you . . . We may not have talked about various things but we've communicated. There's been continuous communication. You can't explicitly discuss everything . . . Tell me about work.

Moira Work?

Roy Your job, occupation, with Dr Godsave.

Moira I like it.

Roy Yes.

Moira It pleases me. As your occupation pleases you, I think.

Roy (*pouring a Scotch, emptying the bottle*) I've taken early retirement.

Moira I know. They rang me to tell me they were worried about you.

Roy It occurs to me that, as a doctor's secretary, you must know a lot about the doctor's patients.

Moira What are you saying?

Roy I'm not saying anything. We've never really discussed your job –

Moira We never really discussed yours.

Roy It occurs to me, that you must know lots of stuff about people that other people not in your job would not know.

Moira Obviously. And?

Roy It must be interesting. And privileged. And is it a little voyeuristic? What would tempt you away from this pleasing position of Dr Godsave's secretary?

Moira You're on the Scotch, now.

Roy I've had a couple. Shall we drink some water?

Moira For the novelty?

Roy Too much red wine and Scotch and I can feel the moisture being sucked out of me.

They drink water.

Moira Doesn't taste of much, does it?

Roy Clean. It tastes clean. Ish.

Moira Where would you find clean water, these days? Rain has to fall through the sky. Is the sky clean? Doubt it.

Roy Some facts about water: most of the earth is water. Rain falls into the oceans or, if it falls on land, it travels to the oceans. The sun heats it and it evaporates and rises and cools and condenses and falls as rain. There is no new water. A dinosaur drank this. And at some point, a fish crawled out of it and climbed a tree and became a monkey, and the monkey became a man, etcetera . . . Water being drunk, what shall we have next? You decide.

Moira Sainsbury's, Safeways, Waitrose or what's this?

Roy Oh that. I thought we were going to run out one night a few weeks ago so I got that from that dodgy, dirty –

Moira draws the cork on the sixth bottle of red.

– dingy off-licence on the corner of Jasmine Road. Plain label: Bulgarian. Eleven per cent.

Moira The cork is relatively clean. It has not absorbed much colour. There are no crystals adhered to it. The colour is reasonable, the bouquet manageable and the taste – mmm – forgivable. (*She tips out nearly all the contents on to the floor, wasting the wine except for half a glass, which she sips.*) Mmmmm.

She offers the half-glass to Roy.

Roy It's all right for you, you've got your Valium.

Moira Would you like some?

Roy I think Valium is generally regarded as a woman's drug. When a man takes it, it's a sign of weakness, but when a woman takes it, it's borne of need. Mmm.

Moira Mmm.

Roy Sometimes one has to drink a primitive red to remind one of the quality of what one may have become complacent over. On TV the other day they showed a journey that recreated the route I took when I was twenty-one, hitch-hiking through France to Spain. St Malo. Le Mans. Poitiers. Bordeaux. Carcassone. Perpignan. Into Spain: Gerona, Barcelona, etcetera, etcetera. I drank wine as a matter of routine. White or rosé at lunchtime with bread and cheese or pâté by the side of the road. Red in the evening. All so cheap and so drinkable. Didn't care where I was or where I was going as long as I headed roughly south. Or south, roughly. A German youth tried to shag me, once. Did I ever tell you that? And the heat. And the noisy insects. There was a forest one night. Pine. Leaking sap. Resin vapour. Dew hanging in the air. It was spring. Moon behind cloud. Glow-worms like cat's eyes. But higgledy-piggledy. Erratic. Lead you off the path. Tried to pick some up to light me the way but as soon as they're in the palm of your hand they extinguish themselves, switch themselves off, or whatever they do. I have clear memories. I can remember where I was, what it smelled like, what it sounded like, what it felt like, what the temperature was, the scent of food in the air, the sound of, of space around me, the smell of heat, of outdoors. The bread. The wine. The light at Biarritz: the Côte Sauvage. Savage all right, and wild. It's like Cornwall with a sheen of sweat.

Moira It's a dream journey, you and the camper van.

Roy I was thinking more along the lines of a Winnebago, actually.

Moira refuses to indulge him.

I tried hovering over Vince, you know.

Beats.

Moira Go on. Please, tell me more.

Roy I tried to intercede by placing myself between him and death. I hovered upright instead of the sort of face-down hovering I'd previously done when I was watching over them all. I hovered upright like a goalkeeper in zero gravity; I spread myself to make myself as big as possible and held my arms out wide and faced death as I imagined it came for Vince, but I was a Scottish goalie . . .

Moira (*ignoring his lapse into joking*) Go on . . . Go on.

Roy When he died, something dragged him away. Some beast with dripping jowls and huge, hunched shoulders, and great claws dangling dripping corpses of the only-just-dead. This beast dragged him –

Moira No, it was gentle. No beast dragged Vince to his death, he floated away, smiling. (*Beats.*) *Toujours la même, la différence.*

Roy Which is?

Moira We even dispute each other's imaginings.

Roy Our remaining children seem to be accusing us of various – what? How would you classify them – errors, mistakes, crimes, misdemeanors, failures?

Moira I've been accused of cruelty to a boyfriend.

Roy To laugh. How terrible. Do you think we killed Vince?

Moira No.

Roy You said that very quickly.

Moira I didn't have to consider my answer.

Roy But your rebuttal was so quick it occurs to me that the question isn't entirely unfamiliar.

Moira Fuck off. Fuck off, you madman!

Roy A nerve, I see a raw nerve, pulsing. Do you think that our youngest son became the dumping ground for the – do you think that it is possible that the lumps in Vince, the blockages in his tissue were the ossifications of our –

Moira Stop it –

Roy – animosity lodged deep in his tissue, our ossified disappointment –

Moira slaps Roy. Roy slaps Moira. It's over in an instant.

74

Moira Are you okay?

Roy Yes. Are you?

Moira Vince was the conduit between us. He was our medium, our crossroads, our prism. Our mantra, if you like – if I'm not straying too much into Sian's territory – but he wasn't victim to 'the ossification of our animosity'.

Roy If we communicated through Vince then some of what passed through him would have been animosity.

Moira's head drops.

What did you ask the Archbishop of Canterbury? Did you ask him to explain what was happening to Vince, how God could allow it, or decree it, even?

Moira Yes; God's hidden his love from me . . . When I was young, I was a person. Then I became your girlfriend, then your wife, incubator, babysitter, nurse, housekeeper, companion. Now I'm a person again. (*touching his face*) I'll compromise with you. It is a sort of beast. You ignore it for long periods. You block it out, but then after it's quietly wreaked havoc, you remember that it was always out there, circling, occasionally glimpsed, on the edge of the darkness . . .

Roy reaches to touch Moira. She stops touching him.

My fantasy is that other people – no – it only has to be one person, looks at me and says to themselves: 'Look at that woman without a care in the world. Look at that vital, radiant woman laughing her tits off.'

Roy When I was young, I was a youth. I was an adventurer, a traveller, an explorer, an –

Moira Mortgage, all paid off. Children, gone or all grown-up. Allegedly. Purpose of marriage? . . . My animals were lamb, brackets, with mint sauce. Scallops, brackets, pan-fried. Snapping turtle.

Roy Snapping?

Moira Touch it and it tries to bite you, That's its reflex. Horny mouth. Like bone. Bite your finger off.

Roy (*trying an old smile*) My third animal was Bambi.

Moira My snapping turtle could rip your Bambi to pieces.

Exit Moira to outside.

Roy Okay. Okay.

Roy reaches to pour a red wine.
Enter Stuart.
Roy can only find dregs in several bottles. He mixes a glassful out of the dregs.
Enter Sian.

Stuart Where's she going? . . . Where's she going?

Roy It falls to us to wash the plates, then. (*He arranges crockery.*)

Stuart Don't do the plates. Do something. Go after her.

Roy's head goes down.

Please, Dad . . . Please.

A noise inside the house. Sian listens at the kitchen door.

Sian She's come back in the other way.

Roy's still moving crockery.

Stuart Good. I told her she shouldn't do anything. I told her that if she thought you'd had an affair with Janey Hudson she was wrong –

Roy stops moving crockery and studies Stuart.

Roy Why did you say that to her?

76

Stuart Because I was worried. That she might think you had.

Roy Why?

Stuart Because –

Sian Shut up, Stuart.

Stuart What?

Sian Shut up.

Stuart shuts up.

Roy Did Mum say something to you?

Sian You two, just stop it –

Roy Me and Stuart have an arrangement whereby we tell each other the truth. Stuart?

Stuart doesn't know what to say.

Fuck me, you are a fucking idiot. Don't ever tell anybody anything ever again.

Stuart goes nose to nose with Roy. The father doesn't flinch.

Stuart If I'm a fucking idiot then that's genetic. (*Exits.*)

Roy I think he's right.

Roy sits again.

Sian Rest. Good idea. (*She massages his shoulders.*) Dad, did your dad love you?

Roy Sian, I know you mean well, but can you take all your psychopathic mumbo-jumbo and stick it somewhere.

Sian laughs.

Actually, stick it up Ben's arse, from whence it surely came.

Sian We want you and Mum to be happy; me and Stuart both want that. When was your last decent sleep?

Roy I really don't remember.

Sian Don't you? Shall I press you? I could work that spot in the top of your head.

Beats.

Roy Okay.

Roy sits up and braces himself. Sian places a thumb in the crown of his head. She presses down, he presses up. A strange sound escapes him.

Sian Good, but relax more. Let whatever it is go rather than trying to push it out.

They try again, for a moment.

Roy Use your elbow.

She does. Roy emits a big, long noise that only stops when Sian stops.

Thanks.

Sian It's a start, just a start. That's the tip.

Roy Did Ben teach you that?

Sian No.

Roy I thought not. I didn't think he'd teach you anything practical. He just messes with your mind. And he's not charismatic, he's just cunning.

Sian Actually, Dad, Ben's a cunt.

Roy Hear, hear. I agree. Ben's a cunt. Hallelujah!

Sian You know, Dad, in your Winnebago, you could be anyone. You can park it up anywhere. Be anyone. Go to a shop, buy all new clothes, throw the old away. Whoever you meet will think the new you is the real you.

Roy I think it'll be a camper van, actually.

Sian You'll survive, and thrive . . . You're not Bambi, you're a lion, a wounded lion . . . You can look for more love.

Roy What d'ye mean?

Enter Moira from inside. Stuart slips in after her.

Moira What happened to your secret eulogy for Vince that the vicar told me not to tell you he'd told me about?

Roy It's still in my pocket.

Moira Does it say we gave him cancer?

Roy No.

Moira Let me look.

Roy hands it over. Moira scans it.

You can read it now, or I will go.

Roy takes it. He tries to read it out loud.

Roy I can't.

He offers it to Stuart and Sian. She reluctantly takes it, and reads:

Sian 'I've never been in a family in my present capacities as husband and father. The family I was in previously, I was a son, which is, I suppose, where I learnt how to be a father. Sometimes, I don't think I've been very good at any of it. As a father, I find it my tendency to want to protect my children, and to be permanently panicking – on a low level – that I am unable to. This fear has come to fruition because in the case of Vince, mine and Moira's second son, third child, I couldn't protect him. It's obvious that I couldn't because he's dead, and his body lies in this coffin. I want to say thank you for being here today to say goodbye to him and your support for this family in time of great need.' . . . I can't read any more.

Roy (*exhibiting documents from Vince's box, continues from memory*) In years to come when all of us are dead who knew him, this will appear to be Vince's life: started this school on this date: this school on this date: passed these GCSEs – five As, two Bs and an unclassified. In History. Had this National Health Service number. Painted this picture – his first: a primitive attempt at a picture of the sun. Died of . . . this, on this date. These are the bones of his life. His actual bones will persist for a long time, beyond his flesh, and his energy – his spirit, his soul – whatever the correct term is which describes the essence of him, leaves an indelible impression on us. The good, the bad, the infuriating, the cruel, and the delightful.

Moira Thank you, Roy.

Sian Thanks, Dad.

Stuart Thanks, Dad.

Moira You'd been through those things (*Vince's papers*) alone.

Roy Yes.

Moira Shall we open another bottle? Champagne, let's have some champagne.

Roy Champagne?

Moira Hidden.

Moira retrieves a hidden bottle of champagne and hands it to Stuart. Sian scribbles something on a piece of paper.

Sian Yes. My, sort of, eulogy. It's my memory of when Vince made me laugh the most he ever did. It's also the

first time we ever admitted to each other that he'd
become a sexual young man. He was eleven. In Virgin
Records some girls were giving him the glad eye – which
he was being slightly coquettish about returning. I nudged
him in the ribs and whispered: 'I think the one in black
has a soft spot for you.' He turned his big, innocent eyes
on me and whispered back: 'A soft spot? Let's hope it's
her vagina.'

None of them laughs.

Moira Well.

Stuart Good on him. (*Opens the champagne and pours
four glasses.*)

Sian God bless you, Vince.

Roy I toast him: a too short but very much marvellous
life.

Sian *and* **Stuart** Hear, hear!

Sian places her paper in the box.

Stuart Okay, this is my story about Vince.

*Sian's paper catches Stuart's eye. He chokes on a
mouthful of champagne.*

Sian's eulogy is entitled, aide-memoire style: 'Vince,
virgin, vagina.'

They all laugh together.

Moira I hope he wasn't a virgin when he died. I toast
him. I hope you weren't a virgin!

Roy Hear, hear!

Sian *and* **Stuart** Hear, hear!

Moira Do any of you know if he was or not?

Sian I don't think he was.

Moira You don't think he was, or you know he wasn't?

Sian I'm pretty sure he wasn't.

Moira Good, because he was fucking gorgeous.

Sian *and* **Stuart** Hear, hear!

Roy Hear, hear!

Moira I'm drunk, now. All that wine and nothing happens; one glass of champagne and I'm almost anybody's.

   Beats.

Stuart Okay. This is me. Vince had this plan. It came about because me and Vince and Little Charlie were in Beeches Wood last autumn when Charlie started asking why the leaves were falling. 'Because it's autumn,' we said. 'What's autumn?' 'A season.' 'What's a season?' 'There are four seasons.' 'What's four?' You get the picture. Vince came up with the idea of: the three of us, hut in wood, pile of encyclopaedias, etcetera, see all four of the seasons, answer all the questions for Charlie . . . Little Charlie's insatiable curiosity . . . And . . . I wish I'd been like Vince at sixteen. I toast you, Vince! I envied you when you were alive and now part of me envies you dead. You died young, before disenchantment set in. But, I'm going to live. I'm going to take Little Charlie to the woods. Pick a tree in winter. Watch it bud in spring. Full canopy in summer. Autumn.

   Beats.

Moira I've got something Vince liked. This photo of our wedding day.

Roy Oh?

Moira Vince said he liked this one because it catches us off-guard.

Roy He said it made him think of Greek mythology, of Prometheus infusing clay with fire to make man. (*Roy has the same photo.*)

Moira When?

Roy The day before he died.

Moira He said when you looked at this photo, you could feel the heat between us. He said that was the heat that made him, and these two.

> *They drink champagne. They look at the photos. They drink. Moira and Roy look at the photos, look at each other, look away. They drink. They look at each other. By mute consent, they recreate their pose in the photograph. It involves touching, which causes a frisson. They hold the pose, complete with smiles . . . Moira breaks it.*

Moira Buy a van. Do your trip.

Roy (*to Moira*) I'll buy a van in the morning. You can come . . . You don't have to decide now . . . If not tomorrow, then you could catch up with me somewhere . . .

> *Moira declines his offers.*
> *Exit Roy to inside.*
> *Beats.*
> *Exit Stuart to outside.*
> *After a while, Moira goes to the window and looks out, towards Dr Godsave's. Sian watches her. Roy appears in the interior doorway behind them.*

Moira Tomorrow . . . Sian. Tell your father – please tell him, whenever you feel is right, that I'm not angry, and I'm not going over there (*to Dr Godsave's*). Tell him – (*She sees Roy, but doesn't let on to Sian.*) – that's all.

Sian grasps Moira and kisses her on the mouth.

Go and look after Stuart.

Exit Sian to inside. Roy watches Moira from the doorway. Perhaps now the low moon comes out from behind a cloud. Moira switches off any lights. Perhaps now the room has streaks of moonlight slanting across it. Roy wills Moira to look at him. She picks up her handbag.

Moira (*still without looking at him*) Thank you, Roy . . . Thank you.

Exit Moira. There's the sound of waves.

End.